Second Edition
Communicating
with parents of
exceptional children

Improving Parent-Teacher Relationships

Roger L. Kroth
University of New Mexico

with Harriet Otteni
Parent Involvement Center
Albuquerque Public Schools

LOVE PUBLISHING COMPANY
Denver · London

Copyright © 1985 Love Publishing Company

Printed in the U.S.A.
ISBN 0-89108-167-4
Library of Congress Catalog Card Number 84-81940

Contents

APPENDICES

TABLES

FIGURES

Acknowledgments

This book was first written about 10 years ago, to give teachers some practical tips on how to improve their communication with parents— with the ultimate goal of helping children grow. Much of what was written then holds true today. But I, too, have continued to grow through experience, research, and the wonderful educators and parents who keep teaching me. You will meet a number of them throughout this revision. I also still enjoy the support of my wife, Jane, four children, and three grandchildren who keep me laughing.

When the time came to get serious about the revision, it was only natural to turn to my friend, Harriet Otteni, for help. Harriet was, and is, coordinator of the Parent Involvement Center in Albuquerque, where we do many of the things described in this book. She coordinated the federal training project that led to the *Strategies for Effective Parent/Teacher Interaction*, a manual for teacher trainers.

We credit many people in this effort. Clare Hummel, Director of Special Education, and Jo Thomason, Assistant Director of Special Education for the Albuquerque Public School System, moved mountains to support the creation and maintenance of the Parent Center after the federal funds ran out. Paula Parks coordinated the demonstration center and developed many of the ideas that are still being carried out. Marcia Bumkens, JoAnn Paroz, and Gwenlynne Pike continue to expand the original ideas as staff members at the Center.

A number of doctoral students from the University of New Mexico extended our knowledge through their research and active participation in the activities of the Center. Jerry Dominguez, Meave Stevens-Dominguez, Lauren Moss, Bobbye Krehbiel, and Janeen Kirk-Taylor made their mark, as did many others who stopped in to contribute in a variety of ways: Joe Sievert, Kay Haney, Suzanne Robinson, Rudy Montoya, Emily Salazar-Marcum, and Betsy Williams.

Many special friends who are professionals in their own areas of the country, and whom you will see sprinkled throughout the chapters of this book, served on an advisory board for the original center. For feedback and guidance we still rely on Ray Dembinski of Northern Illinois, Denny Edge of Louisville, Jennifer Olson of Idaho, Richard Simpson of Kansas, Bill Wagonseller of Nevada, and Kay Hartwell of Arizona State. In addition, Lu Doty, who worked with us and then went to Kentucky to head up Project Enrich—which has trained thousands of teachers in these materials—continues to share with us neat and "whippy" ideas from the field. Of course, we would never have gotten any place without the help of Fran Cordova, our secretary, editor, and friend.

We would especially like to acknowledge the patience and support of a good friend, Stan Love. His gently prodding over the years is sincerely appreciated. Senior Editor Carolyn Acheson, who has been a guiding light and who has the ability to "think" like her authors, also deserves our thanks.

We've been blessed to have so many good friends and contributors to our own growth and development. In turn, we hope this second edition contributes to *your* personal growth and professional relationships.

Roger Kroth
Harriet Otteni

Introduction

Early in the history of the United States, parents saw a need to establish schools. They formed organizations to build schools, raise money, and encourage legislation favorable to their children. Unfortunately, in more recent times school personnel have not seen a need for parents, except as producers of the raw material—children—for the educators to teach.

In many schools contacts with parents have decreased to the point where computer printouts of grades and an open house conducted early in the year represent the major communication between school and home. Concurrently, parent groups have been less supportive of educational systems. Bond issues have failed; adults in the communities have become more critical of pupil performance as measured by standardized tests; public school coaches have been relieved of their coaching duties for not producing winning teams; and educators have been taken to court for their placement procedures.

Parents concerned with special education, however, have been instrumental in passing federal legislation that extends educational opportunities for all children and, specifically, those considered handicapped. Section 504 of the Vocational Rehabilitation Act of 1973 expressly prohibits discrimination against any individual based on a handicap and ensures all handicapped persons of a free appropriate education in the least restrictive environment. Handicapped children

1

now are assured schooling at public expense, as are normal children. in educational programs designed to meet their individual needs. Further, their education is to be integrated with their normal peers to the greatest extent feasible.

To assist states and local school districts in implementing these nondiscriminatory mandates, the Congress in 1975 passed a companion appropriations bill, the Education for All Handicapped Children Act, Public Law 94-142. Although Section 504 outlines the basic guarantees for handicapped students, PL 94-142 specifies how those guidelines should be implemented. *Parental involvement* in the referral, identification, placement, programming, and evaluation phases of each child's individual education is a major thrust of that law.

As individual parents and parent advocacy groups such as the Association for Retarded Citizens and the Association for Children and Adults with Learning Disabilities have continued their political action and have become increasingly knowledgeable and assertive regarding handicapped children's rights, some school people have felt threatened and "on the line." This book takes the stance that parents and teachers should be viewed as partners rather than combatants, that working together is more productive than blaming each other for the child's lack of optimum growth, and that teachers can employ techniques to increase the probability of improved home-school cooperative efforts.

This is not a book of theory. It is a book of techniques, based on the premise that all parents have strengths from which to contribute to their child's education, as well as needs to be met. It is aimed at teachers, particularly special educators, who would like to improve their skills in interviewing or conferring with parents; who might want to work with groups of parents rather than with only single sets of parents; who would like to consider systems of communicating with parents other than the traditional report card; and who are willing to share with parents some of the things they know about how children learn.

Almost all of the information in this book has been obtained by talking with teachers and parents, observing teachers in their work with parents, and holding conferences or group meetings with parents. This attempts to share with teachers techniques that other educators have found to be effective and to suggest new ideas that might be tried. The ideas are meant to be pragmatic. For the practitioner (i.e., the educator) the criterion for continued use should be whether the technique works. Therefore, the procedures employed have to be continually evaluated.

This book has been organized into three sections; however, we recognize that life situations are not necessarily categorical. Thus, the techniques discussed in one section also relate to the others.

Section I: Understanding the Child and Family (Chapters 1-4)

This section lays the groundwork for establishing positive, productive relationships with parents. The conceptual framework is reflected by a strengths/needs model—the Mirror Model for Parental Involvement—for getting parents involved with their child's education to the extent that they have the time, strength, energy, and skill. Some of the commonalities as well as the differences in parents and siblings of special children are underscored by a discussion of the research related to the dynamics of family life with a handicapped child. The critical importance of developing and using good listening skills is emphasized and supplemented by activities for practice. The need to know oneself and to be aware of the role that perceptions and values play in establishing rapport and good working relationships between teachers and parents is pointed out. Teachers who look at strengths as well as needs, who understand how families work or sometimes don't work, and who listen and check perceptions will have little or no trouble relating to the discussion and activities in Sections II and III.

Section II: Information Sharing (Chapters 5-8)

Parents have a legal right to the information the school has about their children—information parents need for planning. Techniques for providing this information to parents are discussed. Various reporting systems are presented. Tips for conducting effective parent/teacher conferences are given. The use of parent groups as a strategy for sharing information is highlighted.

Section III: Problem Solving with Parents (Chapters 9-12)

One of the most interesting and yet perplexing interactions with parents concerns those times when cooperative action is necessary for solving problems. Successful problem-solving techniques depend on success in obtaining and providing information to parents, as well as on the trust and mutual respect that have been established. Strategies for pinpointing problems and techniques for intervening to obtain change are presented.

In one respect, the organization of this book represents a time sequence of normal teacher-parent interactions. First, teachers obtain as much information from parents as is necessary to plan educational programs for their children in their classes. Second, teachers seek to establish early contact that is comfortable and nonthreatening to the parent, using effective human relations skills. Second, teachers give parents the information they need to work cooperatively with the teacher toward common goals for the children. Third, cooperative planning between teachers and parents may prevent, alleviate, or solve many problems that arise during the educational progress of children. Teachers and parents who recognize their roles as complementary rather than supplementary, who approach their interactions enthusiastically and not apprehensively, and who view the relationship as a partnership will usually be rewarded with happy, achieving children and warm, personal feelings of mutual respect.

Parents who have handicapped children need a great deal of positive reinforcement. Teachers who are mature, secure adults can help parents become productive change agents by providing that positive reinforcement. A careful, extensive review of the literature does not lend any support to the game of "parent blaming" as a means of improving a child's performance, so an alternative hypothesis has been adopted: Cooperative home-school programs will accelerate pupils' academic behaviors and decrease undesirable social behaviors.

1

The Mirror Model

By the 1980s most special education programs had made provisions for systematic parent contact. This stemmed primarily from two pieces of federal legislation. The Family Educational Rights and Privacy Act, which emerged in 1974, defined a number of rights to privacy for both parents and their children. The second important piece of legislation was the Education for All Handicapped Children Act of 1975, Public Law 94-142.

Many school districts have always had policies encouraging parent participation in school activities. Some school districts have set aside time for parent conferences one or two times a year. This generally occurs at the elementary school level, though, and parents have often been discouraged from initiating conferences at the secondary levels. Various Title programs have required parent participation in parent advisory groups, even to the extent of hiring personnel and establishing budgets for parent involvement. Most school systems have encouraged organizations such as the Parent-Teacher Association (PTA) or the Parent-Teacher Organization (PTO) to become involved in school programs.

Just how effective these attempts have been in promoting interaction between the significant adults in a child's life remains in question. Some educators have suggested that the federal legislation has caused more problems than it has solved. Some parents have felt that the doors have not been opened as wide as they should be and that educators have used the law to hide behind. Although the legal responsibilities will not be ignored in the various sections of this book, they will generally be regarded as a part of the total program.

The Mirror Model of Parental Involvement was conceived to try to define the parameters of a comprehensive parent involvement program in a public school setting. This model is based on a philosophy that parents are capable of managing most of their own behavior and that they are willing and able to take responsibility for much of their children's growth and development. Nicholas Hobbs (1978) said it well: "Parents have to be recognized as the special educators, the true experts on their children; and professional people—teachers, pediatricians, psychologists, and others—have to learn to be consultants to parents." The helping professions seem to have a tendency to own many of the problems of their clients or patients rather than take the time to help the parents learn to be their own case managers.

ASSUMPTIONS

A number of assumptions were made when the model was conceptualized (Kroth & Otteni, 1983). The assumptions one makes about the conditions that affect parent involvement influence the activities in which one engages as programs are designed. One is certainly entitled to formulate his/her own assumptions, but the following five considerations were recognized as influencing parent involvement in parent activities and in the delivery of service in a large school system (child population of over 75,000). Although these assumptions appear obvious, they are the reality that one must work within.

Money

There will never be enough money to do the things that parents want or professionals can deliver. Finances always force program personnel into choices. Producing videotapes for small groups would be nice, as would providing parents with take-home computers, but few school districts can consider those possibilities.

A therapeutic parent group or counseling usually involves only a few parents and becomes an expensive component. In-depth services for small numbers are often the first things to go in times of a money crunch. Therefore, in developing services, this component must be placed in perspective. In some cases referral to other community agencies is the best solution. Essentially it is a matter of spending the money where one can get the biggest payoff.

Time

Even if money were not an issue, time probably would be. There is seldom enough time to do what one knows how to do. Teacher time to prepare for interaction with parents and to actually call or interview parents is limited. The amount of time that parents have for attending meetings is limited. (Family characteristics and dynamics will be discussed further in the next chapter.)

In most families, setting aside time for parent-child interaction means rearranging priorities. Most professionals think parents of handicapped children should do this, but it is not always practical, for a variety of reasons. The same challenge arises in suggesting that teachers or educators spend more time working with parents. Time is a commodity that must be considered. There is never enough time!

Personnel

These writers make the assumption that there are not—and probably never will be—enough trained people to facilitate interactions between parents and teachers and to train parents in strategies to work more effectively with their children. Even in 1984 many colleges and universities do not offer any courses in parent conferencing or parent counseling (Kroth, Otteni, & Parks, 1982).

This lack of training affects the type of services that can be offered in a community. If personnel are limited, one has to ask how the maximum benefit can be derived from these individuals. Guerney (1969) has proposed that professionals teach their skills to others, such as parents or other professionals, which has a multiplying effect. There is no way the number of professionals who are available can provide direct service to all those who need it.

Heterogeneity of Parents

Most professionals recognize that parents of exceptional children are not a homogeneous group. Still, this assumption is continually being violated by almost everything that is designed for parents. Teachers who are excellent at individualizing programs for children seldom individualize for parents.

At parent meetings it is not uncommon for someone to say, "The parents who should be here for this information are not here tonight." As Bridge (1976) noted, in addition to variables of ethnicity, religion, education, and income, a wide variety of attitudes, values, and child rearing practices must be taken into account. Some people have difficulty recognizing that not all people have the same priorities. Some parents are having a struggle to survive. One mother said, "I have eight children, my husband has shot at me twice, I'm on welfare, and I'm having a hard time keeping clean clothes on my kids and food on the table. I just can't come to your meetings—'sides, I don't have transportation."

Glenn and Warner (1982) have discussed the transitions that have taken place in families from the 1930s to the present. They pointed out the change in family structure over time. Table 1 attempts to highlight some of the changes that might affect interactions between parents and school personnel.

Professionals often act as if structures were the same as they were years ago. The "Ozzie and Harriet" type of family — in which the father went off to work in the morning and the mother stayed home with the two children, a dog named Spot, and a cat named Mitten — represents only about 7% to 10% of the families today (Nadelson & Nadelson, 1980). Only about a third of the children who are labeled behaviorally disordered are living with their original, intact parents (Casey, 1983). In the 1980s over half the children may be living in a single-parent family by age 15 (Black, 1979; Hamner & Turner, in press; Wallerstein & Kelly, 1979; Wattenberg & Reinhardt, 1979).

These factors affect decisions about attending meetings at school. Many conferences, IEP meetings, and staffings are still being held during the parents' work day, when it is hard for parents to attend. In trying times, some parents are afraid to ask for time off for fear of losing their jobs.

Educators have to decide who is to be invited to meetings because of the alternative family constellations that exist. The trend away from the extended family has made it difficult for parents to leave the child and siblings with grandparents or other relatives while they attend meetings.

Table 1
Families — Style and Structure

THEN — 50 YEARS — NOW

	THEN	NOW
Family Composition:	Many members Extended Intact (Ozzie & Harriet)	Few members Nuclear Reconstituted Alternative styles
Family Interaction:	Work, play games, talk together (2-3 hours a day) Intergenerational	Little family work Parallel TV viewing (average 7 hours a day) 15-20 minutes interaction per day
Family Work:	Mainly fathers Family businesses	Both parents (70% of the time)
Neighborhoods:	Much interaction Ethnic Rural/small town	Anonymity Integrated Urban
Education:	Less than one-half finished high school Few went past high school	Most finish high school Many go on to post high school education
Orphanages:	Some	Very rare
Child Abuse:	???	Currently a problem
Divorce:	Rare	Common (over one-half of children will live in single-parent family by age 15)

Parents' educational levels are often discrepant. Some can read and some cannot. Yet, materials that are sent home generally assume that all parents can read at upper high school levels. After doing a readability analysis on handbooks explaining programs and personnel to parents, we found that most of the material was written at the 11th or 12th grade level (Kroth, 1983). "Consent to test and place" forms were also at that level. Some of the pamphlets that were sent home to explain the'services to parents (e.g., diagnosticians, occupational therapy) were written at the college graduate level. McLoughlin, Edge, Petrosko, Strenecky, and

Bryant (unpublished manuscripts) have looked at some of the materials prepared for parents by state agencies and found them often lacking in readability and clarity. One wonders about issues such as *informed* consent if the parents cannot read the materials.

Heterogeneity of parents is a complex factor that can confuse and confound attempts at communication between school and home. Recognizing and attempting to provide for it was an underlying assumption in the development of the mirror model.

Needs/Strengths

A fifth basic assumption in developing comprehensive parent involvement programs was that all parents had *needs*, and all parents had *strengths*. Failure to recognize the strength factor in parents leads one to an automatic mind set—i.e., parents are not capable.

All parents need some basic "things" in order to make decisions about interventions for their children. Although this is required by law, not all parents recognize that it has been provided for them (Dominguez, 1982). A situation in which professionals believe they have communicated clearly with parents and the parents do not recognize that they have been given the information leads to a communication gap (Korsch & Negrete, 1972).

Undoubtedly one can make additional assumptions about the working conditions and the populations under discussion. These, however, are the ones underlying the Mirror Model of Parental Involvement:

1. There will never be enough money to do the things that need to be done.
2. Time will always be lacking for both parents and professionals to work toward desired goals.
3. Even with training programs already in place, there probably will never be enough trained personnel to satisfy parents or staff.
4. Parents of exceptional children are not a homogeneous group and should not be treated like one.
5. All parents of exceptional children have strengths to be used, and all have needs to be met.

The Mirror Model of Parental Involvement (see Figure 1) was developed based on these assumptions and on years of experience teaching and working with teachers and parents in the public schools and

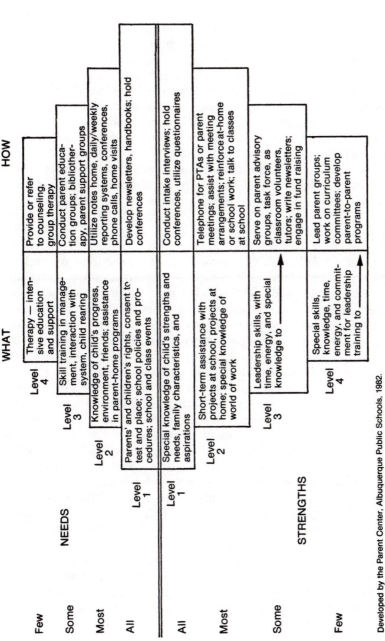

FIGURE 1

Mirror Model of Parental Involvement

Developed by the Parent Center, Albuquerque Public Schools, 1982.

with special interest groups. It is a model for comprehensive parent programs—one that might serve as a guide in planning.

The top half of the model addresses parent *needs*, and the bottom half reflects the *strengths* that parents have. The various levels are an indication that parents are not homogeneous and, therefore, will need to be treated differently. The left side of the model indicates *what* needs and strengths are being discussed, and the right side of the model indicates *how* these might be accommodated with some suggested activities.

All parents do not have the same needs. Therefore, the model has different levels. The assumption is that *all* parents need some things but not all parents need *all* things. The various levels influence the activities that one might find in place in a school system, and they also have relevance for training activities. For instance, the emphasis of this book is on Level 1 and Level 2 activities, because those levels impact the greater number of parents and teachers. This is not to downgrade Level 3 and Level 4 activities but, rather, to put them in perspective.

Needs

Level 4 Needs. One of the most expensive services that a school district can offer to families is therapy. It is time consuming, serves only a *few* families at a time, and usually requires professionals with specialized expertise. Since only a *few* parents need this level of service, the role of school personnel may be that of referral to other community agencies. The percentage of parents needing this service is unknown but probably no more than 5% of the total population of parents. For a large district, however, this could be a substantial number.

Although the segment of parents requiring this level of service is not directly related to the severity of their child's handicap, some professionals believe that parents of severely emotionally disturbed children may need more counseling or group therapy than other parents. This might be related to Bell's bi-directional theory (Bell, 1968; Bell & Harper, 1977), which suggests that not only do adults influence child behavior but children likewise influence adult behavior. Therefore, disturbed children can produce disturbed parents. The ability to recognize the need for help and to match parents with the appropriate community service and make referrals is a competency that school personnel should have.

Another service needed by only a *few* parents a year is a relocation service. Knowledgeable parents realize that not all communities offer the same levels of programs for their children. At the same time, this is a mobile population of adults. Helping parents to check out services and to prepare for the move from one community to another is a service that can be provided to the few parents who need it. Often a couple of phone calls to program directors can clear up questions and concerns before moving.

Some services at this level can be handled by preparing community directories, guides for community services, and other handouts for parents. Getting parents to the right service may be the most important function at this level. In this way, disproportionate amounts of monies are not allocated to Level 4 services.

Level 3 Needs. Parent group work is quite popular, as evidenced in the literature (Cooper & Edge, 1978; Guerney, 1969; Kroth & Scholl, 1978; Rutherford & Edgar, 1979). These writings discuss procedures for designing, implementing, and evaluating parent groups. And many parent programs come in kit form. Only *some* parents take advantage of these offerings. Over time, perhaps 20% of the parents could be expected to attend skill training or support groups. For instance, with a class of 10 children a teacher might expect two or three parents to be willing to participate in three or four sessions of a parent group.

Most of these groups are designed for 10 or fewer participants. Since a teacher or leader is expected to attend regularly to facilitate the group, this becomes an expensive service. Fortunately, many communities have established support groups that are publicized in the newspapers or the yellow pages of the phone book.

For teachers or educators who want to implement parent groups, the commercial materials are often well written, with leader's guides, workbooks, posters, and various supplementary materials. (Some of the programs will be discussed briefly in later chapters.) Most of the programs do require modification for the target populations.

The parent population should be analyzed for the needs that the program should fulfill. At the Parent Involvement Center in Albuquerque, New Mexico, many parent group programs have been developed over the past 5 or 6 years. They have been designed to:

— teach parents to test their own children.
— teach parents to write their own IEPs.
— teach parents to make nutritional snacks.
— teach parents to help their children make the transition between preschool and elementary, etc.
— teach parents to be active participants in conferences.
— teach parents their rights.
— teach parents to be their own case managers.
— disseminate a variety of information/skills.

Parent programs grow out of observed and expressed needs. One can carry out a needs/strengths assessment, or one can become attuned to the needs expressed by parents in everyday contacts. Trained staff members usually enjoy conducting parent groups. They might more profitably use their time to teach others—parents and teachers—to design and run these groups.

Level 2 Needs. Most parents of exceptional children want to know more about the causes of their children's problems, how their children are doing in the treatment programs, and what they can do to help. They usually want this information from the primary source—the teacher, the doctor, the diagnostician—and they want it in understandable terms (Dembinski & Mauser, 1977, 1978).

Since these needs seem to affect about 80% of the parent population, it is important to spend time on how to receive information from parents and how to convey meaningful data to parents. Dembinski and Mauser (1977, 1978) and a series of studies by Korsch (Korsch & Negrete, 1972) have addressed the communication gaps that seem to exist between professionals and parents.

Improving communication between teacher and parent is the primary goal of this book. To this end, attention is paid in these pages to things such as handbooks, handouts, conferencing tips and skills, daily report card systems, and other materials that facilitate understanding between parents and teachers. Computer readability programs have reduced the labor of analyzing materials to the point that sending home any materials that completely miss the mark is almost inexcusable.

Some tip sheets and informational sheets are included as examples in the appropriate chapters and in Appendix B. Another way to consider conveying information to larger audiences is through topical conferences. A variety of general interest presentations has been sponsored by the Albuquerque Public Schools (APS) through the Parent Involvement Center. Topics that seem to be of widespread interest are discipline, divorce, sex education, drugs and alcohol, adolescence, and stress management. Some good materials are available to help in workshops on discipline, in particular (Canter & Canter, 1982; Smith, 1984).

A number of authors have been concerned with the interaction that is meant to occur at Levels 1 and 2 (Coletta, 1977; Kroth, 1975; Lillie & Place, 1982; Seligman, 1979; Simpson, 1982). Parents regard teachers as their primary source of information and support. The more skilled the teacher is in this role, the more satisfaction parents will derive, and the better the programming will be for children.

Level 1 Needs. By state and federal law, *all* parents are to be apprised of their rights and the rights of their children. Since this is a need that affects all children and parents, school district personnel must put some time and resources into activities and materials that explain these rights. Unfortunately, many school district administrators feel apprehensive about conveying this information. Even school districts that are presumably doing a good job in this regard should recognize that their message does not always get across. Dominguez (1982) found that even though school district records showed that parents had signed the various permission slips and forms required by law, these parents reported that they were unaware of what they had done. Further, Williams (1983) found that even when diagnosticians spent a great deal of time explaining test scores and interpretations, parents often were not able to recall the information.

Many school districts prepare handbooks and supplementary materials for parents, but the materials often are not checked for reading levels. A sampling of such materials was found to be at the 10-11 grade reading level, and explanatory material on supplementary services was at the college level. Translating the materials into the parents' primary language (e.g., Spanish) usually misses the mark. The translation is often *textbook* Spanish while the parents may use a combination of Spanish and English (code switching).

Since Level 1 is an area that affects all parents, resources should be put into developing materials and strategies to fulfill the need. Some commercial materials may help, with modifications for any particular population.

Strengths

Level 1 Strengths. All parents know some things about their children or family structure of which professionals need to be aware. Skilled professionals are able to elicit this information through good interviewing skills or observational techniques.

Parents of exceptional children may be working with a large number of professionals. In a weekend camp of families of visually impaired children conducted by Elaine Moses of Region XIII, Austin, Texas, some of the parents were being seen by as many as 20 different professionals, because of the multiplicity of handicapping conditions. This can be overwhelming, because all professionals believe their programs should be carried out. Even well meaning professionals with exemplary programs may produce negative effects on families because the demands of the programs exceed the strengths of the parents (Doernberg, 1978).

Level 2 Strengths. Most parents have the strength, time, and energy to do more than just provide the professionals with information. They may be able to set up a program at home that reinforces what the teacher is doing in the classroom (e.g., reward growth recorded on the child's daily or weekly report card system). Parents might be willing to call other parents as part of a telephone tree, address envelopes, make cookies, or do a number of other one-shot activities. In taking advantage of parents' willingness to help, sensitive teachers allow them to "take a breather" once in a while. Unfortunately, parents who volunteer their services often get overworked. They can get burned out just like teachers, and they don't even get the summer off.

Level 3 Strengths. Remembering the heterogeneity of the parent population, one realizes that some parents have the knowledge, training, and skill to provide training for teachers and other parents. Persons such as Ann Turnbull, Williard Abraham, Helen Featherstone, Doreen Kronick, Kenneth Moses, Judy Zanotti, and Phil Roos have benefited many parents and professionals with their teaching and leadership positions in organizations. This does not mean that they do not have needs of their own, but they are examples of persons who have special talents plus the insights of parents.

Some parents have the time, strength, and energy to assist in the classroom. They may be able to teach children or help teachers. Some may serve on advisory boards or participate in parent panels.

Sometimes parents are asked to participate in roles for which they have not been prepared. This can be unfortunate. If parents are asked to be an aide in the classroom, the expectations should be made clear. If parents are asked to serve on committees or boards, the roles should be clarified and training should be offered if it is needed.

This area of parental involvement is often neglected. Parents represent a rich source of assistance for the welfare of children and a help to professionals and other parents. Not using a parent who has writing skills and the time to help with newsletters and handbooks is a disservice to both the parent and the professional.

Level 4 Strengths. Parents have long been recognized as the major sources of strength for other parents. A number of parent support groups have been formed. For instance, a group in Albuquerque, Parents Reaching Out (PRO), is made up of parents who provide support for each other, produce a newsletter, keep an eye on legislation, provide speakers for interested groups, and are generally available for the unique services that parents need from time to time. A number of communities have the Pilot Parent program.

Recently a Parent Support Network was formed in New Mexico to train parents and professionals to develop support services in their own communities. The strategy of combining parents and professionals from the same community for training was deliberate. Often, parents attend meetings and garner many good ideas, but when they return home, they have no place to meet, no access to equipment, no phones. Professionals may be able to offer these resources.

Large communities have support groups available. These often have a minimum amount of professional assistance. School personnel could help parents locate these groups. The number of parents who are not aware of organizations such as the Association for Citizens with Learning Disabilities, the Association for Retarded Citizens, or the Association for Gifted and Talented Students is surprising. Support groups such as Recovery, Parents Anonymous, and Tough Love are active in many communities.

SUMMARY

The Mirror Model of Parental Involvement provides the parameters of a comprehensive parent involvement program. It carries with it the assumptions that there is not enough money, time, or trained staff to do everything that could be done, so one has to work within these constraints. It also assumes that parents are a heterogeneous group and that each should be treated as an individual, with unique strengths and needs.

The top half of the Mirror Model addresses parent *needs*, and the bottom half the *strengths*. These are depicted in four levels each, ranging from the strengths and needs of just a *few* parents to those of *all* parents. The left side of the model indicates *what* the strengths and needs are, and the right side gives some suggestions on *how* these might be accommodated through various activities. The reader will be able to generate additional activities for each level.

The Mirror Model provides the conceptual framework from which to analyze and formulate comprehensive parent involvement programs. Figure 2 gives a sample analysis form that can be used to check an existing program or to utilize in planning a new one.

REFERENCES

Bell, R.Q. (1968). A reinterpretation of the direction of effects in studies of socialization. *Psychological Review*, 75, 81-95.

Bell, R.Q., & Harper, L.V. (1977). *Child effects on adults*. Hillsdale, NY: Erlbaum.

Black, K.N. (1979, January). What about the child from a one-parent home? *Teacher*, pp. 24-28.

Bridge, R.G. (1976). Parent participation in school innovation. *Teachers College Record*, 77(3), 366-384.

Canter, L.,& Canter, M.(1982). *Assertive discipline for parents*. Santa Monica, CA: Harper & Row.

Casey, R. (1983). *The relationship between school performance during residential treatment and post-discharge school adjustment of emotionally disturbed children*. Unpub-

	OFTEN	SOMETIMES	SELDOM	PRIORITY	PROJECTED START DATE	PERSON(S) RESPONSIBLE
1. Provides written information on consent to test.						
2. Provides written information on consent to place.						
3. Provides written information on criteria to place.						
3. Provides written information on criteria to place.						
4. Provides written information on due process procedures.						
5. Provides written information on availability of child's records.						
6. Has regularly scheduled conferences.						
7. Involves parents in planning the IEP.						
8. Has a newsletter.						
9. Has parent information group meetings.						
10. Uses daily/weekly report cards.						
11. Makes home visits.						
12. Has class handouts.						
13. Makes phone calls systematically.						
14. Uses "good news" notes.						
15. Interprets test results.						
16. Arranges skill training parent workshops (behavior modification, PET (Parent Effectiveness Training), problem solving).						
17. Takes family history						
18. Elicits child strengths from parents.						
19. Conducts parental needs and strengths assessment.						
20. Has "room" parents.						
21. Has parents assist on field trips, parties, etc.						
22. Has parent advisory groups.						
23. Has parent volunteers in the classroom.						
24. Involves parents in special interest task forces (curriculum, discipline, needs and strengths assessment).						
25. Uses parents as co-partners for other parents.						
26. Uses parents as workshop leaders.						
27. Other:						

Developed by the Parent Center, Albuquerque, NM

FIGURE 2
Parent Involvement Program: Analysis Sheet

lished doctoral dissertation, University of New Mexico, Albuquerque.

Coletta, A. (1977). *Working together: A guide to parent involvement.* Atlanta, GA: Humanities Unlimited.

Cooper, J.O., & Edge, D. (1978). *Parenting strategies and educational methods.* Columbus, OH: Charles E. Merrill.

Dembinski, R.J., & Mauser, A.J. (1977). What parents of the learning disabled really want from professionals. *Journal of Learning Disabilities, 10*(9), 49-56.

Dembinski, R.J., & Mauser, A.J. (1978). Parents of the gifted: Perceptions of psychologists and teachers. *Journal for the Education of the Gifted, 1*(2), 5-14.

Doernberg, N. (1978). Some negative effects on family integration of health and educational services for young handicapped children. *Rehabilitation Literature, 39*(4), 107-110.

Dominguez, J.C. (1982). *The effects of training on special education teachers' perceptions, knowledge, and interactions with parents.* Unpublished doctoral dissertation, University of New Mexico, Albuquerque.

Glenn, H.S., & Warner, J.W. (1982). *Developing capable young people.* Hurst, TX: Humansphere, Inc.

Guerney, B.G. (1969) *Psychotherapeutic agents: New roles for nonprofessionals, parents, and teachers.* New York: Holt, Rinehart & Winston.

Hamner, T., & Turner, P. (in press). *Parenting in contemporary society.* Englewood Cliffs, NJ: Prentice-Hall.

Hobbs, N. (1983). Classification options: A conversation with Nicholas Hobbs on exceptional child education. *Exceptional Children, 44*, 494-497.

Korsch, B.M., & Negrete, V.F. Doctor-patient communication. *Scientific American, 227*, 66-74.

Kroth, R. (1975). *Communicating with parents of exceptional children.* Denver: Love Publishing Co.

Kroth, R. (1983). *A readability analysis of selected handbooks and materials written for parents.* Unpublished manuscript, University of New Mexico, Albuquerque.

Kroth, R., & Otteni, H. (1983). Parent education programs that work: A model. *Focus on Exceptional Children, 15*(8), 1-16.

Kroth, R., Otteni, H., & Parks, P. (1982). Parent involvement: A challenge for teacher training institutions. In M. Peters & N. Haring (Eds.), *Building an alliance of children, parents and professionals* (pp. 181-205). Seattle, WA: Program Development Assistance System, University of Washington.

Kroth, R., & Scholl, G.T. (1978). *Getting schools involved with parents.* Reston, VA: Council for Exceptional Children.

Lillie, D., & Place, P. (1982). *Partners: A guide to working with schools for parents of children with special instructional needs.* Glenview, IL: Scott, Foresman & Co.

Nadelson, C.C., & Nadelson, T. (1980). Dual-career marriages: Benefits and costs. In F. Pepitone-Rockwell (Ed.), *Dual career couples.* Beverly Hills, CA: Sage Publications.

Rutherford, R.B., & Edgar, E. (1979). *Teachers and parents: A guide to interaction and cooperation.* Boston, MA: Allyn & Bacon.

Seligman, M. (1979). *Strategies for helping parents of exceptional children.* New York: Free Press.

Simpson, R.L. (1982). *Conferencing parents of exceptional children.* Rockville, MD: Aspen Systems Corp.

Smith, D.D. (1984). *Effective discipline: A positive approach to discipline for educators in all settings.* Austin, TX: Pro-Ed.

Wallerstein, J.S., & Kelly, J.B. (1979, November). Children and divorce: A review. *Social Work,* pp. 468-475.

Wattenberg, E., & Reinhardt, H. (1979, November). Female-headed families: Trends and implications. *Social Work,* pp. 460-466.

Williams, B. (1983). *Diagnostician-parent communication.* Unpublished doctoral dissertation, University of New Mexico, Albuquerque.

ACTIVITIES

1. Analyze your own program using the form provided (page 18).

   a. Is your program comprehensive?
   b. Which things might you work on first?
   c. List the things that are in your community if not in your own program.

2. By reviewing your records and personal knowledge, analyze the parents in your class or program.

   a. What are the needs for each parent, as you see them?
   b. What are the strengths?
   c. Do you spot any parent(s) who you think might be utilized to help other parents?
   d. How heterogeneous is your parent population?

3. Generate activities that could fit at different levels of the Mirror Model.

4. Design a comprehensive parent involvement program for your class/community.

2

Family Dynamics

"I just found out my son is handicapped."
"Oh, I'm sorry. I know just how you feel."
"Do you have an exceptional child?"
"No, but . . . ."

In attempting to be helpful, many people try to suggest that they know how parents of a handicapped child feel. But unless one has been there, it is not possible to have the same feelings. Even the parents do not have the same reactions to the birth or identification of a handicapped child. Two parents with a similar experience may perceive it differently.

Barnlund (1976, pp. 716-717) said, "All knowledge of the world is inescapably subjective....Each of us views the world selectively and fits it to our own past experience and changing purposes." Therefore, when parents of handicapped children—such as Elaine Moses and Reed Martin—share experiences, they may have a great deal of understanding of each other, but they undoubtedly differ in some of their feelings after filtering their messages through their own past experiences, emotions, and thoughts.

21

One must be continually reminded that parents are not a homo geneous group. A parent who has had a retarded brother may view the advent of a retarded child much differently than a parent who has had virtually no experience with exceptional children or adults. When and how the child was diagnosed, how severe the handicap is, the visibility of the handicap, where the child is in the family constellation, and the culture and the mores surrounding handicapping conditions influence parents' feelings. These variables and many others affect a family's perception of a handicapped member and influence the reaction to that individual.

Despite these differences, most parents and professionals report some similarity in the reactions that parents have when a child is diagnosed as handicapped. Therefore, some understanding of what may be going on will aid teachers as they work with the parents in parent involvement programs, IEPs, and other activities.

THEORIES OF PARENTAL REACTION _____

Two theories or theses that explain parents' reactions to the realization that their child is handicapped are discussed here. Both theories address the same observable behavior, but they define it in different ways.Probably the best known is the *psychological stages* point of view. A lesser known viewpoint is that of *chronic sorrow*.

Psychological Stages

Solnit and Stark (2961) proposed a theory of mourning that would result from giving birth to an imperfect child. They suggested that parents (particularly the mother) use certain defense mechanisms to protect themselves from psychological damage. These mechanisms are considered to be healthy and normal.

Elizabeth Kubler-Ross (1969) is probably best known for her book on *Death and Dying*. In an interview (Kubler-Ross, 1981) she said, "You have to understand I did not learn this from dying patients. I learned it from all my years of working with blind people and multiple-handicapped, retarded patients, first in Switzerland and then here." Duncan (1977) adapted the stages of death and dying described by Kubler-Ross in "grief theory" to handicapped populations. Various authors (Buscaglia, 1975; Moses, 1979; Stewart, 1978) have expanded upon these stages. They have been proposed as developmental stages.

Stage 1—Denial

Any time a traumatic event that involves a loss occurs, the first reaction is shock, followed by denial. This may occur over a wrecked car, a divorce, the death of a loved one, or the birth or diagnosis of a handicapped child. It is like saying, "If I don't pay any attention to it, it might go away."

When a teacher has to tell parents that their child is failing or should be referred for special testing, the parents may act as if they did not hear. They may ignore the advice, or they may go shopping for another diagnosis. The denial stage *is* productive, although the professionals may feel that time is being wasted. It is a time that gives the parent some space to think about and absorb what is being presented.

Many professionals believe that this is the most frustrating stage for both parents and professionals. Parents may claim they were never told certain things, when the professional knows they were (Korsch & Negrete, 1972; Williams, 1983). Professionals may feel personally rejected, when the parent is actually rejecting the diagnosis. Parents may think that the professionals are not being honest. Each may become impatient with the other. Parents may resent the bearer of bad news, as in the days of yore when the messenger bringing the bad news was put to death.

Although the psychological stage theory is viewed as being developmental, many parents report going in and out of denial depending on the external environment. One mother said, "Every time we change schools, I think that maybe if I don't say anything about it, they won't notice."

As long as the denial stage does not drag on, it is considered to constitute a safe reaction. Besides, the search for new information may be warranted (Hollingsworth & Pasnaw, 1977). Professionals often find that time and patient, nonjudgmental repetition of information are key concepts in working with parents at this stage.

Stage 2—Bargaining

During this stage the parents have accepted the diagnosis somewhat, but they have not accepted the prognosis. It is a stage in which a parent says, "If I work hard, my child will get well." Parents are willing to try a variety of cures, with the hope that one of the programs will prove successful.

Many parents throw themselves into high levels of activity in organizations. Again, this reaction is not unhealthy. In many ways it can help control anxiety and make parents feel productive. It also can be helpful to the total cause of services for handicapped children.

Stage 3—Anger

Anger can take a variety of forms and have a variety of targets. Since being angry at a handicapped child is not socially acceptable, the rage is often taken out on someone else (Moses & Kreidler, 1981). A teacher may wonder why a parent who has been so cooperative is suddenly angry with the program being laid out or the services being offered. Persons who are not aware of this reaction to the frustrations and anxiety of having a handicapped child might get caught up in conflict. A professional may display strong resentment when what is really needed is some quality listening.

The anger does not always go away. Moss (1981) interviewed parents of learning disabled adults. Quite a few of them were still angry, because programs were not available for their children when they were in school and services were inadequate in the transition from school into the world of work.

During this stage mothers may fight with fathers, and both may fight with siblings. Siblings may feel a great deal of resentment toward their handicapped brother or sister. These feelings may lead to feelings of *guilt*. As with the other stages, patience, understanding, listening, and maybe counseling can be helpful. To retaliate with anger is seldom beneficial.

Stage 4—Depression

Feelings of guilt and inadequacy associated with traumatic situations often lead to feelings of depression. The handicap does not go away. The parents have tried a variety of programs and have received second and third opinions, and the child is still handicapped.

Since most adults have gone through some traumatic event in their lives, they will recognize the feelings that parents have during this stage. Parents may feel both hopeless and helpless and, as a result, may seem paralyzed with inaction. From a professional's point of view, this is a difficult stage to help parents through. Encouragement often seems to fall on deaf ears. Too much sympathy may provide secondary gain. Professionals often report that they would rather deal with parents' anger, because at least there is a response with which to work.

Stage 5—Acceptance (Coping)

The final stage is usually described as one of acceptance, but some authors (Featherstone, 1980; Moses & Kriedler, 1981) tend to view it as coping rather than acceptance. As Featherstone pointed out, "There is nothing final about acceptance....The most important difference between mourning a death and mourning a disability is that the child in question is not dead at all....While death provides a moment's respite from ordinary demands, disability generates new tasks and necessities" (pp. 231-234). At any rate, this stage reflects coping behaviors that suggest the parent has come to grips with the reality of the handicap. It is important, however, for the parent to maintain hope. This can be the driving force that keeps people going (Cousins, 1981). As a parent once said, "The difference between professionals and parents is that professionals want to talk in terms of probabilities and parents want to talk about possibilities. It is the *possibility* that keeps us going."

The psychological stage theory of grieving seems to suffer somewhat by the implication that parents move neatly from one stage to another and finally arrive at a stable state of acceptance. Reality seems to dictate a different pattern. Many parents report that they never denied they had a handicapped child; in fact, they had a hard time getting a professional to confirm their diagnosis. They were the ones to first identify a problem. Also, many parents report having reexperienced some of the stages as their child reached certain milestones, such as moving from middle school to high school. In this respect these healthy defense mechanisms seem to be used periodically throughout the child's and parents' lives.

Chronic Sorrow

The second theory or point of view suggests that the grieving process is not time-bound but, rather, continues throughout the lives of the parents and child. Both theories recognize the initial shock that occurs at diagnosis, but the difference is in the explanation of the subsequent events and feelings (Wikler, Wasow, & Hatfield, 1981).

If one accepts the chronic sorrow viewpoint, the implications are that parents need support throughout their lives. This suggests that a continuum of services should be provided and that parents will need information appropriate to the stage the child is in, to alleviate the sorrow. Since parents are being encouraged to keep their children at home as opposed to institutionalization, professionals must recognize the need for continual programs available to parents in the community.

Well adjusted parents become anxious when children reach certain educational or life change levels. For instance, parents who have fought long and hard for educational programs often become dismayed when their children are no longer eligible for educational programs and they see few offered in the community. Anger resurfaces and depression is common, with little apparent acceptance.

Regardless of the theory one chooses to adopt, parents obviously go through trying times. Familiarity with these theories and stages will help the teacher react in appropriate ways (Kroth & Krehbiel, 1983).

PARENTAL AWARENESS

Because of the defense mechanisms just described, a number of professionals have been concerned about parents' level of awareness of their child's handicapping condition. If parents deny the handicap, how accurate are parents as reporters of their child's performance?

Upon early identification the mother and father are regarded quite frequently as the primary informants. A social worker or a diagnostician has an intake conference to obtain relevant information. Sometimes the parent is asked to respond to the items on the Vineland or other testing instruments.

Zuk (1959) studied what he called the *autistic distortions* in parents of retarded children. He used the term in the context of "a process which causes a person to see what he wishes to see." (p. 171). In addition to Zuk, a number of researchers have tackled the problem, using a variety of strategies. Salazar-Marcrum (1982) reviewed many of the studies (see Table 2).

The population most commonly investigated was that of mentally retarded children. Most of the time, the comparison focused on intelligence. In some cases, parents were asked to estimate their children's abilities; in other studies they were asked to take tests as they thought their children would take them. In the latter case, they might actually take the test and respond as their children would, and in other situations they might just be asked to indicate whether they thought their children could answer the items. Some studies were concerned with the children's self-concept.

In general, the mothers often scored their children higher than the children's actual tested scores, although the differences were not always statistically significant. Whenever self-concept was the issue, the

Table 2
Parents' Estimation of Their Exceptional Children's
Potential, Ability, or Self-Concept

Who	When	Exceptionality	N	Age	Measure	Strat-egy*	Corre-lation**	RESULTS Difference
Ewert & Green Stern	1957	MR & Organic	100	X=6.4 Range 1-4 to 14-6	IQ	1	r=+.55	Tested IQ=44.1 Significant Est IQ=58 testing not reported.
Schulman & Stern	1959	MR	50	X=5.8 Range 3-3 to 12-10	IQ	1	r=+.67	Tested IQ=55.5 Not significant Est. IQ=57.2
Zuk	1959	MR & MR w/ Motor Impair-ment	145 22	Range 1-8 Range 1-8	IQ	2	N.R.	Parents significantly higher w/MR. Parents not significantly higher w/MR with motor impairment.
Jensen & Kogan	1962	CP			Achieve-ment	6		Mothers estimated higher than staff ratings—more so with physical than intellectual.
Capobianco & Knox	1964	MR	66	X=11-7 5-2 to 17-6	IQ	3	N.R.	Mothers significantly higher than both child and father.
Barclay & Vaught	1964	CP	40	20 6 20 6	Rating of future	2	N.R.	Mothers significantly higher than investigators.

*Key to strategies:
1. Mothers were asked to estimate the age at which child functions in general.
2. Parents informing on Vineland and compared to tested IQ.
3. Mothers (and/or fathers) were asked to respond as they thought their child would.
4. Mothers and teacher were asked to fill out the developmental profile.
5. Mothers were interviewed with adaptations of the Bailey Scale (infants) and the McCarthy Scale (preschoolers) and compared with diagnostician's actual results.
6. Parents and teachers were asked to fill out a rating scale for comparisons.

**All correlations significant at .05 level.

Table 2
Parents' Estimation of Their Exceptional Children's Potential, Ability, or Self-Concept
(continued)

Who	When	Exceptionality	N	Age	Measure	Strategy	Correlation	RESULTS Difference
Mathaney	1966	MR	30		IQ	1	r=+.83	Tested 59.2 / Est. 66.0 — Significant testing not reported.
Gorelick & Sandhu	1967	MR	25	X=7.4 / 3-6 to 15-6	IQ	3	N.R.	Tested X=51.8 / Mother X=57.7 (significant difference)
Heriot & Schmickel	1967	BD	65	X=7.9 / 1-4 to 14-9	IQ / Vineland	1	r=+.49	Tested X=77.3 / Mothers X=80.8 (significant difference) / Mother/tested not significant.
Piers	1972	Normals / Clinic population	188 / 97	8-14	Self-concept	3	N.R.	Normal parents agreed and estimated significantly higher than child. / Clinic mothers estimated significantly lower than child.
Sexton, Kelley, & Scott	1982	MR, OH, Autistic, etc.	18	X=3.7 / 0-7 to 6-0	LAP	3	r=+.95	Mothers higher than examination but significantly higher on only one subscale (gross motor).
Gradel, Thompson, & Sheehan	1981	Mixed handicapping conditions	60	30 / 3-24 mo. / Infant / 30 / 38-78 mo.	Development	4 / 5	4=.415-.868 (Infant) / r=+.95-.98 (Preschool) / r=+.686-.666 (Infant)	Mothers significantly higher than teachers, both infant and preschool. / Mothers significantly higher than diagnostician evaluation.

Table 2
Parents' Estimation of Their Exceptional Children's
Potential, Ability, or Self-Concept
(continued)

RESULTS

Who	When	Exceptionality	N	Age	Measure	Strat-egy	Corre-lation	Difference
Salazar/ Marcrum	1982	LD	20	8.9 to 14.0	Achieve-ment	3	r=+.613 (reading/ math) r=+.452 (spelling)	Mothers tended to estimate higher than actual performance all tests except self-concept, which was estimated significantly lower.
					IQ		r=+.613 (verbal) r=+.599 (perform.) r=+.689 (full)	
					Self-concept		r=+.243	Not significant

mothers usually felt that their children had lower self-concepts than the children reported they did. The results of the parents' scores, when correlated with the tested results, were statistically significant and often highly correlated.

From the results of the studies, the question of parental awareness of their child's handicapping conditions might be answered in a number of different ways.

1. Perhaps the mothers know best. Tests usually represent a sampling of behavior taken at a particular time. The mother has a larger time sample from which to draw.
2. Even when the mothers' scores are higher than those the investigators elicit from the children, the scores usually are still in the intelligence range of the target population.
3. The discrepancy may reflect the parents' need for *hope*, or the *possibility* of performance and achievement that are needed in order to keep searching for success.
4. Parents are a heterogeneous group. Some may be accurate and good informants; others may not.
5. These studies did not include parents of "normal" children (with the exception of the Piers study). Therefore, we cannot know whether these are typical parent/child reactions in the general population.

The results do not suggest that parents' views should be rejected. In fact, the parents may be right and the tests may be wrong. It might be a good idea to ask parents what they think the results of a test will be before starting to interpret it to them. In any case, being on the high side is healthier than being on the low side. Many teachers feel that parents who have "given up" are extremely difficult to involve.

EFFECTS ON THE FAMILY

The effects of a handicapped child on the family structure are difficult to assess. Part of the reason for this is the lack of baseline data in general. Some parents report that the birth of a handicapped child has strengthened their marriages and brought the family closer together; others report the opposite (Freeston, 1971; Kolin, 1971; Walker, Thomas, & Russell, 1971).

The diagnosis of a handicapping condition will certainly have some effect on the family. Schedules will be altered, finances affected, interpersonal relationships and time for each other changed. Even in today's world parents will often have to move to communities that have programs suitable for their children. This may mean that the father or mother has to take a lesser job. Even in an enlightened 1984 relatives can put a lot of stigma-related pressure on the parents. Recently a mother of a visually impaired/mentally retarded child related that her inlaws would not even acknowledge her child.

Therapy may take away time from the other children or from the mother and father. One mother reported that she had done "everything you professionals told me to do. I took my child to speech therapy, physical therapy, a special preschool, and worked with him in the evenings and on weekends. In the process I forgot I had a husband — and one day I didn't." Another mother living in a rural area had to take her severely handicapped child to a large city two or three times a week. On one of the trips, her "normal" daughter was with her because the mother could not get a sitter. The daughter asked her mother, "Are you ever going to have time to play with me again?"

In an effort to begin to get some baseline data for comparative purposes, the following was collected about a behavior disordered population:

1. In a typical classroom one might expect one of five (20%) of the children to be living in a one-parent family. For comparison, the Albuquerque Public Schools, in an ongoing study of children in classes for the severely behaviorally disordered, has found that about 45% were living in single-parent families or some living arrangement other than the traditional two-parent family. This finding differs significantly from the "normal," learning disabled, and gifted populations in the same community.

2. Casey (1983) found that 22% of the children being admitted to a residential treatment center for emotionally disturbed children were living with both natural parents, and 71% were living in single-parent families.

3. A study that is still ongoing in the Albuquerque Public Schools indicates that only about a third of a random sample of behaviorally disordered children are living with both natural parents, a fifth with a parent and a step-parent, and the remainder in some other living arrangement.

These data would imply that, at least with families of behaviorally disordered children, the composition is different from other families. These data do not answer the question of whether the child's behavior affects family relationships or family relationships affect the child's behavior. Perhaps it is enough to recognize that, in either case, parent involvement with the schools will be affected.

SUMMARY

When a handicapped child is born into a family or diagnosed at a later date, the event is traumatic and has an effect on the family dynamics. From one point of view, the event is regarded as the "death" of a normal child and the parents go through a period of mourning. The *psychological stages* of this process are predictable and are similar to the stages described by Kubler-Ross (1969) in *On Death and Dying*. After the. initial shock, parents can be expected to progress from *denial* to *bargaining* to *anger* to *depression* to *acceptance (coping)*. In reality, parents probably go in and out of these stages from time to time depending on external conditions.

Another point of view is that of *chronic sorrow*. After the initial event and the subsequent shock, parents are considered to be continually affected by the child's handicap. As Moss (1981) pointed out, the parents still may be angry years later. And as Featherstone (1980) commented, the difference is that the child does not die.

Although parents tend to estimate their children's potentials higher than standardized evaluations, parents' scores correlated highly with the professional evaluations and generally were in the range of scores of the handicap being studied. This substantiates the position that parents should be regarded as a valuable source of information.

The birth or diagnosis of a handicapped child affects family dynamics and family structure in several ways, involving finances, schedules, time demands, and interpersonal relationships. Professionals' awareness of this impact should lead to realistic requests for parental involvement.

REFERENCES

Barnlund, D.C. (1976). The mystification of meaning: Doctor-patient encounters. *Journal of Medical Education, 51,* 716-725.

Buscaglia, L. (1975). *The disabled and their parents: A counseling challenge.* Thorofare, NJ: Charles B. Slack, Inc.

Casey, R. (1983). *The relationship between school performance during residential treatment and post-discharge school adjustment of emotionally disturbed children.* Unpublished doctoral dissertation, University of New Mexico, Albuquerque.

Cousins, N. (1981) *Human options.* New York: Berkley Publishing Corp. (1977).

Duncan, D. (1977, May). *The impact of a handicapped child upon the family*. Paper presented at the Training Model Session, Harrisburg, PA.

Featherstone, H. (1980). *A difference in the family. Life with a disabled child*. New York: Basic Books.

Freeston, B.M. (1971). An inquiry into the effect of a spina bifida child upon family life. *Developmental Medicine & Child Neurology, 13*, 456-461.

Hollingsworth, C.E., & Pasnaw, R.G. (1977). *The family in mourning: A guide for health professionals*. New York: Grune & Stratton.

Kolin, I.S. (1971). Studies of the school-age child with meningomyelocele: Social and emotional adaptation. *Journal of Pediatrics, 78*, 1013-1019.

Korsch, B.M., & Negrete, V.F. (1972). Doctor-patient interaction. *Scientific American, 227*, 66-74.

Kroth, R.L., & Krehbiel, R. (1983). *Parent-teacher interaction* Washington, DC: *American Association of Colleges for Teacher Education*.

Kubler-Ross, E. (1969). *On death and dying*. New York: Macmillan Publishing Co.

Kubler-Ross, E. (1981, May). Interview. *Playboy*, p. 76.

Moses, K.L. (1979). Parenting a hearing impaired child. *Volta Review, 81*, 73-80.

Moses, K., & Kreidler, K. (1981). *Bridging the gaps*. Springfield, IL: Association for Retarded Citizens.

Moss, L. (1981). *A descriptive study of learning disabled adults and parents of learning disabled adults*. Unpublished doctoral dissertation. University of New Mexico, Albuquerque.

Salazar-Marcrum, E. (1982). *Mothers' perceptions of the learning disabled children's learning disabilities and self concept*. Unpublished doctoral dissertation, University of New Mexico, Albuquerque.

Solnit, A.J., & Stark, M.H. (1961). Mourning the birth of a defective child. *Psychoanalytic Study of the Child, 16*, 523-537.

Stewart, J.C., (1978). *Counseling parents of exceptional children*. Columbus, OH: Charles E. Merrill Publishing Co.

U.S. Bureau of the Census. (1983). *Household and family characteristics: March 1982* (Current Population Reports, Series P-20, No. 381). Washington, DC: U.S. Government Printing Office, 1983.

Walker, J.H., Thomas, M., & Russell, I.T. (1971). Spina bifida—and the parents. *Developmental Medicine & Child Neurology, 13*, 464-476.

Wiklei, L., Wasow, M., & Hatfield, E. (1981). Chronic sorrow revisited. Parents vs. professional depiction of the adjustment of parents of mentally retarded children. *American Journal of Orthopsychiatry, 51*(1), 63-70.

Williams, B. (1983). *Diagnostician-parent communication*. Unpublished doctoral dissertation, University of New Mexico, Albuquerque.

Zuk, G.H. (1959). Autistic distortions in parents of retarded children. *Journal of Consulting Psychology, 23*, 171-176.

ACTIVITIES

1. Convene a panel of parents. Prepare a list of questions for them to respond to, such as:

   a. effect on siblings.
   b. inlaw reactions.
   c. changes in their life styles.
   d. financial and other difficulties.

2. Read selected articles in the *Exceptional Parent* magazines.

3. Read book(s) by parents of exceptional children from the list of Suggested Readings (page 35).

4. Interview one or two parents (develop a structured or semistructured interview protocol).

5. Analyze the family composition of the children in your class.

SUGGESTED READINGS

For Children

About Handicaps (1974)
Sara Bonnett Stein
Walker & Company
New York

Anna's Silent World (1977)
Bernard Wolf
J. B. Lippincott Company
Philadelphia and New York

More Time to Grow (1977)
Sharon Hya Grollman
Beacon Press
Boston

My Brother Steven is Retarded (1977)
Harriet Langsam Sobol
Macmillan Publishing Company
New York

Parenting and Handicapped Children

A Difference in the Family (1980)
Helen Featherstone
Basic Books/Harper & Row
New York

A Parent's Guide to Learning Disabilities (1978)
Alice D'Antoni, Darrel Minifie,
& Elsie Minifie
Continental Press
Elizabethtown, PA

Can't Read, Can't Write, Can't Talk Too Good Either (1973)
Louise Clarke
Penguin Books
New York

Hope for the Families (1973)
Robert and Martha Perske
Abingdon Press
Nashville, TN

Human Options (1981)
Norman Cousins
Berkley Publishing Corp.
New York

Parents Speak Out (1978)
Ann and H. Rutherford Turnbull
Charles E. Merrill Publishing
Company
Columbus, OH

Raising a Hyperactive Child (1973)
Mark A. Stewart and Sally Wendkos Olds
Harper & Row
London, England

So Your Child Has Cerebral Palsy (1975)
Gil Joels
University of New Mexico Press
Albuquerque

Something's Wrong with My Child (1979)
M. Brutton, S. Richardson, & & C. Mangel
Harcourt-Brace-Jovanovich
New York

Son-Rise (1976)
Barry Neil Kaufman
Harper & Row
New York

Words for a Deaf Daughter (1976)
Paul West
Harper & Row
New York

You Always Lag One Child Behind (1980)
Willard Abraham
Sunshine Press
Scottsdale, AZ

Compiled by the Parent Center, Albuquerque, NM

3

Listening to Parents

To be human is to speak. To be abundantly human is to speak freely and fully. The converse of this is a profound truth, also: that the good listener is the best physician for those who are ill in thought and feeling. (Johnson, 1956, p. 20)

One of the quickest ways of receiving information from parents is to have a meeting in which the parents feel comfortable in expressing themselves freely and openly. Also, as Johnson (1956) pointed out, a good listener provides an atmosphere that is especially profitable for problem solving. In a conference the teacher who is a good listener receives a tremendous amount of information, both verbally and nonverbally, from parents. In turn, parents are able to solve many of their problems by discussing them with a teacher who is a good listener. Therefore, developing good listening skills is important.

A LISTENING PARADIGM _____

Sometime during the teen years individuals tend to get classified as listeners or nonlisteners by their peers. This classification is not to be equated with the classification given children by teachers. Some children whom teachers have identified as nonlisteners, or who do not appear to pay attention in class, are viewed by their peers as very good listeners in a one-to-one relationship.

The individuals we are talking about here are those whom others seem to seek out to talk over problems. They often are not the cheerleader or top athlete types, but they are socially sensitive people. They are usually interested, concerned, caring individuals who tend to be nonjudgmental. Their listening posture ranges from a passive, attending manner to one of becoming actively involved in the feeling content of the messages of others.

On the other hand, a large number of individuals may be characterized as nonlisteners. They may be highly verbal, able to give clear directions or commands. They may advise, preach, and lecture, or they may withdraw and be more interested in things and ideas than in listening to people. Their nonlistening posture ranges from a passive, nonattending manner to one of becoming actively involved in *talking* about the nonfeeling content areas of the other person's messages. Figure 3 is an attempt to place the various postures into a listening paradigm.

No individual, of course, is in any one of the quadrants all of the time. A person may shift from quadrant A to B or from B to D in any conversation. In fact, one can sometimes observe passive listeners (A) slip into a passive nonlistener (C) role by watching their eyes get that faraway look. Each of the four quadrants will be discussed briefly.

1. *Quadrant A—Passive Listening.* The passive listener is "there" and "with it." In a conference this teacher can think out loud with the parent, who usually feels confident that what is said will stop in that room. The passive listener may give a number of nonverbal signs of acceptance such as a leaning forward, nodding the head slightly, and smiling, that let the parent know that it is all right to talk. Often the parent is surprised that he/she could talk so much or that so much time has passed.

   A teacher who is not a passive listener but who would like to try to become one will probably find the role uncomfortable at first. Nature seems to abhor a vacuum, and the teacher can usually fill the silences that occur faster than the parent can. In fact, it might be well to practice on the teachers in the teachers' lounge before venturing on to the playing field.

2. *Quadrant B—Active Listening.* Authors such as Dinkmeyer and Carlson (1973) and Gordon (1970) have been concerned about the role of the active listener—one who is actively involved in helping another person identify and clarify his/her problems, beliefs, and value system. In many respects the active listener can be equated to an excellent dancing partner; he/she seems to feel the rhythm of the conversation and moves accordingly.

Nonverbally, the active listener probably leans forward and maintains more than the usual amount of eye contact during a conversation (Knapp, 1972). Verbally, this teacher reflects back to the parent the feelings he/she hears expressed and may try to reverbalize important and complex statements with, "I think I hear you telling me..." to test his/her perceptions. This type of listening is hard work, and often the teacher and parent feel emotionally drained after such a session.

In Bersoff and Grieger's article "An Interview Model for the Psychosituational Assessment of Children's Behavior" (1971), the initial interviews with parents seem to involve an active listening posture on the part of the interviewer. The model would appear to encompass the skills of the nondirective counselor for uncovering the problem areas perceived by the parent—

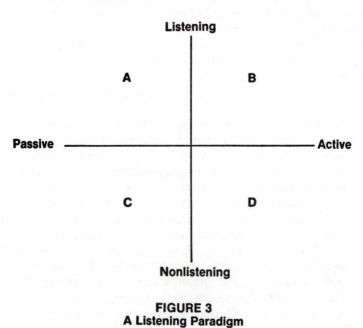

FIGURE 3
A Listening Paradigm

i.e., identifying the target behavior, the situations in which the behavior occurs, the consequences that maintain the behavior, and, in addition, the skills of the behavioralist in setting up a plan for analyzing and modifying the target behavior.

One of the major strengths in active listening is that it keeps the problem where it belongs—with the parent. The teacher does not take over the problem by offering solutions or make the parent feel guilty by moralizing. The active listener does try to clarify the problem and help the parent put it in perspective. The book *Parent Effectiveness Training* (Gordon, 1970) gives more information about active listening.

3. *Quadrant C—Passive Nonlistening.* The passive nonlistener often seems to "hear" what is being said but is not involved in listening to the feeling content of the messages. This posture can be frustrating to the one who is trying to communicate with another person.

Wife: I'm so tired. I've been to four stores today trying to find material for a new dress. You're not listening!

Husband: (folding the newspaper): You said you've been to four stores looking for material for a new dress.

Although the content was accurate, the husband missed his wife's feelings of fatigue and frustration. She really could not argue that he was not listening, because he was able to parrot back most of her words accurately; however, no real communication took place. These are two people physically in the same room, one who is trying to send messages to alleviate some of her feelings and the other who is submerged in his own thoughts.

A similar situation occurs in some parent-teacher conferences, particularly when a number of conferences are being held in succession. The teacher may be physically meeting with Mrs. Smith, while her mind is on a conference she is soon to have with Mr. Wilson. She looks at Mrs. Smith. She is able to repeat many of the words if called upon, but as far as the conference is concerned, she is a passive nonlistener.

When an adult's mind slips out of its listening gear and starts to pursue its own thoughts, children sometimes tug on his/her clothes, a reminder of the lack of listening. Parents seldom tug, but they probably are aware when the teacher's own thoughts take over. The teacher who is "with it" probably should stop the conference, inform the parent that he/she is preoccupied with a pressing matter, and perhaps suggest getting together with Mrs. Smith on another day. Being honest with a parent at this point will probably help build good relations for future conferences.

4. *Quadrant D—Active Nonlistening.* There are at least two types of active nonlisteners and a number of variations of the two. One type of active nonlistener is the Cocktail Party Type, and the other is the Wipe-Out Artist.

Almost everyone has had the experience of being at a social gathering where a great deal of talk was going on, with virtually no listening. In this type of conversation, people talk *to* each other but seldom *with* each other.

Mrs. Smith: We're so glad you could come. I heard you were out of town.

Mrs. Jones: We just got back. We were attending my aunt's funeral in California.

Mrs. Smith: California is so pretty this time of year. We were at Disneyland last spring. I enjoyed it so much.

Mrs. Jones: We were in Albuquerque last spring. Oh, there's Ruby. I must tell her about the squash blossom necklace I found.

Neither person is particularly interested in what the other person has to say. Usually each waits politely for the other to finish a sentence and then talks. This type of behavior is fairly easy to recognize in social gatherings. It is a little more difficult to observe in a parent-teacher interaction, though it is probably just as prevalent. Often parent and teacher enter a conference with something to convey to the other. They talk for 20 minutes and separate, neither having attended to the other's message.

Teacher: I'm so glad you could come. I've been wanting to talk with you about Billy.

Parent:	I'm having trouble getting Billy to do his homework. He always wants to put it off, and we have frightful arguments around the home.
Teacher:	He's been fighting on the playground. I've had to keep him in from recess twice this week.
Parent:	I don't think he understands the new math. That's probably why he doesn't do his homework. I wish you could do something about it.
Teacher:	Do you have any idea why he's started fighting so much? Does he ever talk about it at home? We just don't know what to do with him. It's getting to be a real problem.
Parent:	We're having a real problem, too. We're open for any suggestions. This arguing is getting both his Dad and me upset.
Teacher:	We at school want to cooperate in any way we can. If you have any ideas about fighting, call me, will you? It's sure been nice talking to you, and I'm so glad you could come. You're always welcome at school.
Parent:	I'm happy to have met you. If you have any ideas how we can help at home, just call. We want to work with the school.

This type of conferring probably happens more often than one would like to believe. Both parent and teacher are trying to communicate and cooperate, but they are not taking the time to listen to what the other has to say. In the above, little is accomplished, but both leave feeling that at least they have had their say about their problems.

The Wipe-Out Artist is probably the most exasperating type of active nonlistener. This type of nonlistener unravels the outer threads of the story and never allows the theme of the story to be unfolded. He/she appears to be actively attending but actually reacts to the incidentals of the message. This can be especially frustrating if one is trying to relate a situation in which one is emotionally involved or feels strongly about. Either the parent or the teacher may act as a Wipe-Out Artist during a conference.

Parent:	Billy had the neatest thing happen to him on his way home from school.
Teacher:	How does he go home from school?
Parent:	Down Center Street and ——
Teacher:	Isn't that past the fire station?
Parent:	Yes, and ——
Teacher:	Last year five of our boys said they wanted to be firemen when they grow up. What does Billy want to be?
Parent:	A nuclear physicist.
Teacher:	Isn't that cute? And to think he can't even spell it. What happened to him on the way home?
Parent:	Well, he ran into this man who ——
Teacher:	I hope he said "excuse me." We stress good manners in our room. We have a unit on the magic words—*please* and *thank you.* I hope you notice the improvement at home.

With a little practice almost anyone can become an expert in active nonlistening.

People do not fit neatly into one of the four quadrants. Most move from quadrant to quadrant depending on the situation. There is probably a propensity to be consistently more of one type than another, though. A good way to analyze one's behavior is to tape-record an interview and listen to it.

DETERRENTS TO LISTENING _____

A number of things can happen before or during a conference that may slow down or temporarily stop communication. The listening behavior of one or both of the participants may be reduced to the point where the conference is no longer profitable. From the teacher's point of view, here are six deterrents:

1. *Fatigue.* Listening is work. If the mind or body is tired, one will be a much poorer listener. We all have had the experience of sitting in lectures when we have been so tired that we cannot mentally follow the speaker. If the teacher has a number of conferences in a row and has really worked at listening, his/ her mind will be wandering toward the end of the day. A break should be scheduled to walk around and perhaps have a cup of coffee.

2. *Strong Feelings.* At times a particular child evokes strong feelings of anger because of some behavior. A cooling-off period may be in order before having a conference with the parents. This could be a time when the teacher would want to talk to the school counselor about his/her own feelings. Other strong feelings, including sadness and happiness, can make listening difficult. Taking stock of oneself before entering into a conference with a parent is wise.

3. *Words.* The children's verse that ends, "but words will never hurt me" is far from true. Consider for a moment the impact of the following:

> "You're fired!"
> "I'm pregnant."
> "Your child is retarded."
> "This is the police."
> "I love you."

The very words one uses or hears can make the pulse beat more rapidly, sweat appear, and the eyes dilate. The teacher must carefully consider the words he/she uses with parents and realize that certain words may deter or end listening on the parent's part.

In discussing with parents of exceptional children the effects of the conference when a diagnostic label was applied to their child, many indicated that they heard nothing after being informed that their child was "retarded" or "emotionally disturbed." Parents apparently go through a series of psychological reactions such as shock, denial, guilt, rejection, blame, anger, embarrassment, and hostility before they accept the diagnosis and begin the productive steps of habilation (see chapter 2 for further discussion). Teachers who recognize that parents are having a difficult time adapting to the reality of having a handicapped child allow the parents every opportunity to talk over their feelings as these feelings relate to the child.

Realizing that parents, just like teachers, may enter a conference with "strong feelings" (point 2), the teacher should not be surprised if certain words used during a conference may end listening on the part of parents. When this happens, the teacher might suggest that parents take some time to think about what was discussed and then set a date in the near future to continue the conference.

4. *Teacher Talk.* A high percentage of teacher "talk time" in a parent-teacher conference reduces the amount of listening time. A teacher once asked to have a tape of one of her parent conferences critiqued. By using a stopwatch, it was determined that the teacher had talked 80% of the time during the conference. If, as Wendell Johnson (1956, p. 23) says, "... we come in time to realize that every speaker is his own most captive listener," the teacher probably learned more about how *she* felt about the child than the parents learned about how they felt about the child. Basically, she spent very little time in listening to the parents and allowing them to listen to themselves discuss their child. A teacher does need to "listen to himself/herself" by talking about a child at times, but this is best done by talking to a listener other than the parent. The above mentioned conference was probably more therapeutic for the teacher than for the parents.

The time that the teacher engages in talking during a conference reduces the time that can be spent in listening. If listening is considered important, it is wise to analyze the time participants of conferences spend in talking.

5. *The Environment.* The physical surroundings can have an effect on listening. With a great deal of distraction, attending to another person—either visually or auditorially—is difficult.

Even a parent's physical comfort can have an effect on the interaction.

> A businessman once had two chairs in his office for people who came to see him. On one chair he cut two inches off the front legs, and on the other chair he cut two inches off the back legs. If he wanted the interview to be short, he put the client in the chair with the front legs shortened; if he was in no hurry, he seated the client in the chair with the short back legs. Merely controlling the seating arrangement seemed to have the desired effect.

6. *Writing.* Writing during a conference is a controversial issue. With some parents writing seems to inhibit the flow of conversation; with other parents it seems to increase the conversational flow. Many professional people (e.g., doctors, lawyers) take notes during an interview. Also, something about writing seems to help the listener focus on the messages being relayed. Perhaps this is more true when the listener is fatigued than when he/she is alert. Students sometimes say that taking notes during a boring lecture is one way of keeping their attention focused on the subject.

Many things can affect listening behavior in parent-teacher interactions. By becoming aware of the deterrents to listening, teachers can work on improving their listening skills. At the end of this chapter are some activities that may improve one's listening ability.

SUMMARY

Listening serves the important purposes of (1) receiving information from parents and (2) helping to solve problems—and thereby having a therapeutic effect on the person being listened to. Since listening serves these important functions, it is well to assess oneself as a listener.

Listeners in a communication interaction can be classified according to four types. One is the *passive listener*—the individual who attends to the speaker primarily on a nonverbal level. The *active listener* seems to work at helping the speaker clarify his/her thoughts, attitudes, and feelings about the subject being discussed. The *passive nonlistener* does not attend to messages on a feeling level, although he/she may be able to repeat words that were spoken during the interview. The *active nonlistener* appears to take "equal time" in any conversation, possibly with material unrelated to the basic discussion. On a more difficult level, the active nonlistener may pick at the threads of a conversation and seemingly avoid the central issue being discussed.

Teachers should be aware of deterrents to listening, although they may not always be able to control them. Fatigue on the listener's part reduces listening effectiveness. Either the parent's or the teacher's strong feelings may affect the interview adversely. Words themselves have a tremendous effect if they are emotionally laden. Excessive talk by the teacher reduces the time that he/she has for listening. The physical surroundings can either distract or enhance an interview. The issue of writing during a conference is unresolved.

Listening is a skill that can be improved by practice. The activities at the end of this chapter may be helpful.

REFERENCES

Bersoff, D.N., & Grieger, R.M. (1971). An interview model for the psychosituational assessment of children's behavior. *American Journal of Orthopsychiatry, 41,* 483-493.

Dinkmeyer, D., & Carlson, J. (Eds.). (1973). *Consulting: Facilitating human potential and change processes.* Columbus, OH: Charles E. Merrill.

Gordon, T. (1970). *Parent effectiveness training.* New York: Peter H. Wyden.

Johnson, W. (1956). *Your most enchanted listener.* New York: Harper & Brothers.

Knapp, M.L. (1972). *Nonverbal communication in human interaction.* New York: Holt, Rinehart, & Winston.

ACTIVITIES

1. Role-play or conduct an actual conference. Video or audio tape the interview. Play back the tape and, using a stopwatch, record how many minutes you talked. Time the length of the interview, then divide the number of minutes the interview took into the number of minutes you talked, to find the percentage of "teacher talk time."

2. In a class or workshop on parent conferences:

   a. Divide the class into groups of three.
   b. Have one member in each group think of something exciting to relate; designate the second member as an *active nonlistener*; and ask the third member to be an observer. Have members 1 and 2 role play for 3 minutes and then spend 2 minutes discussing their feelings in the small group.
   c. Then have member 2 think of something exciting to tell, and have member 3 be an *active listener* and member 1 the observer. Have members 2 and 3 role play for 3 minutes and then spend 2 minutes discussing their feelings in the small group.
   d. Reassemble the small groups for a class follow-up discussion:

      —Discuss feelings related to the different listening styles.
      —Discuss nonverbal signs of communication.

      Give each person the opportunity to be a speaker, listener, and observer.

3. Practice active listening skills in your classroom during group discussions.

4

Perceptions and Values

"How was school today?"
"Fine."
"What did you do?"
"Nothing."
"Why are you an hour late?"
"I had to stay after school."
"Why?"
"For throwing rocks on the playground."

Messages go home from school every day via thousands of little messengers. Sometimes the day's events are shared verbally, and other times they are transmitted nonverbally. A tear-stained face, torn jeans, a paper with a star or "happy face"—all are messages that parents receive daily. From these bits of information parents paint whole pictures of their child at school.

MISPERCEPTIONS AND ASSUMPTIONS _____

Sometimes the father paints a picture quite different from the mother with the same bits of information. The father might interpret torn jeans and a low score on a math paper as "all boy—a chip off the old block," while the mother may read the same signs as "poor little boy—he was picked on by school bullies, and the teacher doesn't help him with his work." In the meantime the teacher may be thinking, "I'm glad Billy did the work himself today. That's the first low score in math he's had in the last month, but I think he understands how to work the problems now."

The messages that children bring to school are no more complete than the ones they take home. Forgotten homework, the same shirt four days in a row, only candy bars for lunch, and yawns are signs that the teacher sees and interprets in drawing his/her picture of the child's home life.

> Phil was an engaging frecklefaced kid with a big smile. He was one of the shortest boys out for basketball, but he seemed to make up for size with a lot of enthusiasm. His gym shirt looked as if it belonged to a big brother, and his tennis shoes were held together with broken shoestrings.
>
> The coach took a special interest in Phil because of his personality more than his basketball ability, and kept him on the basketball team for that reason. Concerned about Phil's decrepit "uniform," the coach began looking into ways to get him a decent pair of basketball shoes to replace the tattered tennis shoes.
>
> Discussing the situation in the teachers' lounge one day, one of the teachers asked the coach what the boy's last name was. When the coach told him, the teacher laughed and said, "Why don't you call up his dad and ask him to buy Phil a new pair? He's the manager of Miller's Department Store."

This incident is just one example of misinterpreting messages from home to school. Jumping to conclusions or making assumptions based on very little evidence is probably more common than one would like to think. Being right in one's assumptions occasionally is probably reinforcing enough for one to keep making assumptions. One can check out assumptions in a number of ways. Probably the simplest is to telephone the parents and ask!

VALUE ASSESSMENT AND CLARIFICATION

Many factors influence one's perceptions, the quality of a parent-teacher interaction, the process, and ultimately the outcome. Each participant brings to the exchange certain physical, emotional, and behavioral characteristics and past history, which all affect the individual's perception of the world. These characteristics may be considered as *inputs,* and they have a potential effect on all interactions. In some cases these characteristics may generate such strong feelings that two individuals may not be able to enter into a working relationship. One of the major factors affecting the parent-teacher relationship is the value system of each of the participants.

The values that both parents and teachers bring to interactions have been developed over the years through personal interchanges and relations with others, reinforcement histories, and contemplation. Because these values are so basic to each person, they are not often brought to the surface for reexamination. Knowledge of one's own values and the values of those one is working with can help alleviate potential conflicts.

Contrary to the opinions of many critics, we are not living in a valueless society; nonetheless, to generalize about group, societal, or individual values is becoming increasingly difficult. Since we are a mobile people and have access to radio, television, movies, magazines, and other reading material, we have discovered numerous alternative styles of behaving. Trying to generalize a value system across a segment of people is no longer profitable. To say that "Teenagers believe," "Chicanos value," "Blacks think," "Teachers regard," or, "Parents consider" will probably miss as many who fall in the designated category as it will hit. A city official in a small town once said, "The way to get along in this community is to pay your bills on time, hold your liquor well, and engage in your extracurricular affairs very discreetly." Although these guidelines may have a ring of truth to them, many people living in small towns do none of the above, manage to get along very well, and may be some of the most important persons in the community.

Teachers, counselors, or consultants (these labels can be used interchangeably because all are considered to be teachers of new understandings and skills to significant others) are faced with two major undertakings. The first is to understand or clarify their own value system. This is perhaps the first major step in seeing ourselves as others see us. The second is to try to understand the value system of the person that is being taught or to help the other person understand his/her own value system.

The Importance of Understanding Values

The importance of assessing one-s own values or attempting to understand another's values is that ultimately one tends to act on the values that are the most cherished. Literature and history are filled with numerous value dilemmas and conflicts. On a lesser level, the dilemma may involve the decision of an overweight person to eat a hot fudge sundae or a lettuce salad, or that of a classroom teacher to grade students' papers or watch TV, or a parental decision to play with their child or go to a cocktail party.

Understanding one's values is important because people often do not act on objective information. Logic would suggest that the dieter standing nude on a scale in front of a full-length mirror with a calorie counter in hand would choose the lettuce salad over the hot fudge sundae. And logic prevails, right? Wrong! As another example, a review of research indicates that employing a daily or weekly report card system has a positive effect on children's academic and social growth (Dickerson, 1972; Edlund, 1969; Fuller, 1971; Kroth, Whelan, & Stables, 1970; Simonson, 1972); yet, many special education teachers do not use such a system in their classrooms. Graphs and charts as a tool to measure child progress in the classroom have been shown to be effective in evaluating teaching techniques, but many teachers abandon the practice when they are no longer involved in research projects or coursework requiring this or when they leave a practicum experience.

Value systems are complex and individualistic. The churchgoing citizen who drives ruthless business bargains during the week but shuns the town drunk or prostitute who tries to attend church raises the cry of "hypocrite." The client-centered counselor who uses behavior management techniques is viewed as a Judas. The behavioralist who engages in active listening or values clarification exercises is regarded as having feet of clay. The better one understands one's own and others' value systems, the fewer judgments one is likely to make about apparent inconsistencies in behavior.

Values Clarification

The values clarification movement has enjoyed a great deal of popularity from the mid-1960s to the present. Sidney Simon is probably the best known in this area. He has co-authored a number of books that explain the concept and outline strategies for clarifying values (Raths, Harmin, & Simon, 1966; Simon, Howe, & Kirschenbaum, 1972; Simon & O'Rourke, 1977). Other books, such as *Discovering Your Teaching Self*, by Curwin and Fuhrmann (1975), provide exercises for teachers to use to clarify their teaching values and examine their behavior in the classroom. Interestingly, the popularity of the movement chronologically parallels the popularity of the behavior modification movement in American education circles.

According to Simon et al. (1972, p. 20) "...the values clarification approach does not aim to instill any particular set of values." A number of strategies are provided to help participants gain a clearer idea of what values or behaviors they choose, prize, and are willing to act upon. Some of the activities are to be done individually; others are intended for groups.

The movement is not without its critics. Stewart (1975) has pointed out a number of dangers, including what he perceived to be a degree of superficiality in values clarification. Since some of the strategies call for a public affirmation of values, he noted that group pressure could have an effect on individuals who are highly susceptible to peer approval. In addition, because of the way that some values are presented, they appear to have a negative connotation, so that even if one holds a particular position, one may hesitate to publicly admit it. In a similar vein, if one were to succumb to peer pressure and publicly support a value that peers held, one might feel compelled to act on that value rather than changing later. As in most methodologies, (e.g., behavior modification, T groups, and transactional analysis) the key to the success of any technique is the sensitivity of the person applying that technique. The potential user of value clarification methodology would be well advised to read the critique by Stewart (1975) as well as the literature supporting values clarification.

One can use many values clarification activities that safeguard individual feelings and that provide an opportunity for introspection. If trust has been established between parent and teacher, the results of the activity can be shared, leading to increased understanding by both parties. Some of these activities are presented in Appendix G. Additional strategies are included in the books referenced at the end of this chapter.

Those who utilize values assessment techniques are moving into a sensitive area. Governmental agencies have answered the demand for increased respect for the privacy and well-being of individuals. Although conscientious teachers automatically respect the rights of others, one should also remember that these rights are protected by law, specifically the Family Educational and Privacy Rights Act of 1974.

Self-Assessment of Values

As a counselor once said, "If I don't know who I am and where I'm coming from, how can I help someone else discover this about himself?"

If one accepts the premise that a teacher, counselor, or consultant is going to teach another significant adult in the child's life the means of understanding and intervening, it is important to apply these techniques to oneself.

A good review of techniques for assessing the self is "Self-Conception Methodologies," in *Studies in Self-Cognition: Techniques of Videotape Self-Observation in the Behavioral Sciences* (Geertsma & Mackie, 1969). Techniques ranging from free response to fixed response strategies are discussed. Some of the results may be analyzed by looking at the responses to questions such as "Who Am I" or at the completion of "fill-in-the-blank" sentences. Others have elaborate scoring systems.

Selected activities that might help one reflect on one's own value system are given in Appendix G. In some cases, they have been adapted from existing strategies or assessment techniques. Few can be considered completely original, as finding a technique that has not already been tried is difficult. When possible, the original source has been cited.

COMMUNICATION GAPS _____

Recently, two doctoral students were implementing a parent project. They were interested in what parents remembered from a test interpretation session. They videotaped all the procedures so they could review what was said and compare this to what was remembered. One of the parents—usually the mother—took the test in the way she thought the child would, and then the child took the test. After the tests were scored, the doctoral students developed graphs, charts, and other interpretative aids to help explain the results to the parents. The interpretation sessions were lengthy, to be sure that the parents' questions were all answered.

At the end of one of the sessions, Betsy Williams, one of the doctoral students, asked the parents if they had any more questions. Both parents assured her that they understood everything perfectly. They said they appreciated the information and thanked her for her time. On the way out, Emily Salazar-Marcrum, the other doctoral student, met them at the door and asked them how the interpretation went. Did they understand everything? She asked them what they had learned. The father replied, "Well, I learned that my son has a reading disability." The mother looked at him in surprise. "No he doesn't."

They had both heard the same message, been videotaped, assured the professionals that they understood and had no more questions. Yet they had heard two different messages!

The above example is not uncommon. Most people have had similar experiences. They have seen or heard something and then disagreed on what occurred. *Selective perception* means that one hears or sees what one expects to see or hear or what one chooses to perceive. Usually this is based on one's past experiences. As Barnlund (1975) said, "Each of us views the world selectively and fits it to our own past experience and changing purposes.... Since every interpretation of events rests on fallible senses and personal motives, what is known is always incomplete and always subject to error" (p. 717). This is one of the reasons that parents and professionals often disagree on what was said in a conference. Korsch has been interested in this phenomenon and conducted studies in which she taped the communications between doctors and patients. Some of her findings are found in Figure 4.

The findings from Figure 4 translate easily to teacher-parent interactions. For instance, the use of jargon is not the sole prerogative of the medical profession. Educators, too, have their own language. Even though parents may nod their heads as if in agreement, much is lost in the translation. In analyzing tapes of parent–teacher conferences, teachers are commonly found to talk most of the time. The attitude toward parents must be related to the effectiveness of the interaction. Also, at the conclusion of a staffing for a child, more than three recommendations are often given. If patients fail to comply when three or more prescriptions are offered, parents could well fail to comply if educators' recommendations are too numerous.

DELIVERING SENSITIVE INFORMATION _____

Doctors, psychologists, and educators frequently have been criticized for the insensitive manner in which they have informed parents of "bad news." Although professionals may not like the criticism, it should not come as a surprise, nor should they become defensive about it. Few professionals have been taught or trained to deliver sensitive information. As a result, some are evasive, some are blunt, some are authoritative, some employ jargon, and most talk without listening.

Barnlund (1976) has listed 10 obstacles to communication that become exacerbated when the issue or topic is sensitive. The obstacles are: ego involvement, differences in knowledge, social status, communicative purposes, emotional distance, one-way communication, verbal manipulation, ambiguity of language, role of jargon, and the pressure of time.

1. Korsch, B.M., & Negrete, V.F. (1972). Doctor-patient communication. *Scientific American, 227,* 66-74.

Analysis of audiotaped pediatrician-parent/patient interactions in the outpatient clinic of a large urban hospital; 76% of the parents felt satisfied with their pediatrician's communications. Further findings:

1. 20% had no idea what was wrong with their child.
2. 50% had no idea of the cause.
3. 38% complied only in part with pediatrician's recommended treatment.
4. 11% did not comply at all.
5. No correlation existed between length of visit and patient satisfaction or clarity of diagnosis.
6. Language was much too technical—physicians resorted to medical jargon.
7. Severest complaint of dissatisfied mothers was that physicians had shown little interest in their great concern about the child.
8. 26% of mothers told interviewers they had not mentioned greatest concern because they did not have the opportunity or were not encouraged; this often resulted in a complete breakdown in communication.
9. Patient rapport and cooperation thrived on specific instructions.
10. Verbatim records showed that on the average the doctor did more talking than the mother.
11. Doctor's attitude toward mother mattered more than attitude toward child.
12. Friendly treatment of patient generally had favorable results; harsh treatment tended to yield poor results. There was a direct statistical relationship between the amount of nonmedical (social) conversation between doctor and patient and the patient's satisfaction.

The major finding was that when the doctor was perceived as unfriendly or as *not* understanding, compliance decreased. Physicians were perceived as too technical in their language. The major complaints, however, were that the physician showed a lack of concern and interest or was not interested in the mother's report.

2. Vida, F., Korsch, B., & Morris, M. (1969). Gaps in doctor-patient communication. *New England Journal of Medicine, 280,* 535-540.

Findings:

1. When three or more medicines were prescribed or both medicine and treatment were prescribed, overall compliance was reduced.
2. A longlasting relationship increases compliance.

Perceived lack of friendliness, failure to meet expectations on diagnosis, and lack of demonstrated understanding of parent/patient concerns were all positively correlated with noncompliance of patient with physician treatment.

FIGURE 4
Most Common Problems in Communications
Between Physician and Parent

The following story may provide an example of some of the obstacles.

> About 20 years ago, a Native American mother gave birth to a child with Down syndrome. At the time, these children were often referred to as mongoloid. The doctor said to the mother,"You have a mongoloid child. Do you know what that means?" Not wanting to sound unknowledgeable or challenge the doctor's position, the mother nodded. When she took the baby home, she visited with her own mother.
> "Mother, do you know what a mongoloid child is?" she asked.
> "I think it's somebody from Asia," her mother responded.
> "I wonder how I got an Asian child," the mother thought.
> Mrs. C. related this story a few years ago to illustrate how she was told about her handicapped child, and how she had been taught to have such respect for doctors that she did not ask questions or for more information.

All people have to receive and give bad news in the course of their lives. This may be something as simple as telling one's mate that a favorite vase has been broken to informing someone that his/her mother or father has died. With relatives, usually the giver of bad news has considerable background information on the receiver of the bad news. This knowledge allows the sender an opportunity to pick the most conducive time and place for whatever discussion will be needed.

Watching a child pick the time and place to inform a parent of a bad report card is interesting. The child may go to great lengths to prepare the environment, and these preparations alert the parent that something is going on. "I wonder what Billy is up to?" Likewise, when a parent goes into the child's room and closes the door, messages are being sent to the child about the news that is coming. In our personal relationships we learn a great deal about communication with each other if we tune into the verbal and nonverbal messages that are being transmitted.

Joan Guntzelman, a counselor at a hospital, works with patients and their relatives who need help coping with the situations of terminal illness, serious operations, or feelings of helplessness. She stresses that people who convey bad news or sensitive information differ in their styles and that each person should find techniques that are comfortable to him/her. Some of her suggestions for delivering sensitive information to parents are summarized in the listing.*

1. Provide a comfortable environment. Privacy affords the opportunity for the parent to react according to felt needs.

---

*Adapted from remarks by Joan Guntzelman, Counselor, Presbyterian Hospital, Albuquerque, NM

2. Tell the parents together, if possible. When one parent has to tell the other, misunderstanding and confusion can result.
3. Be aware of the readiness level of the parent to receive the information.
4. More information may be communicated through nonverbal cues than by what is said.
5. Try to have some sense of what the diagnosis means to the parents.
6. Keep the information simple and basic.
7. Try to communicate a sense of being calm and composed. Try not to communicate feelings hastily. Allow time for questions from the parent.
8. When delivering bad news, don't give the "heaviest" information during the first visit. The rapport established during the intake interview will be helpful.
9. Do not argue with denial. Denial may be part of the process in the parent's accepting a handicapping condition.
10. Try to be honest and straight without being brutal.
11. Avoid jargon, whenever possible.
12. Be accepting of parents' reactions.
13. Be aware of one's own need for power and control in the conference or situation.
14. Depending upon the degree of difficulty expected, allow sufficient time for information to be communicated.
15. Be aware that parents may not process all the information given them.

Many times the school environment is used to convey bad news to parents. This atmosphere can be sterile and foreboding. Sometimes the recipient of the news has had a history of bad feelings about the school environment stemming from his/her own childhood. A counselor's office or the principal's office may be better than either the teacher's classroom or the teacher's lounge. Privacy is often limited in a classroom, and certainly is limited in the lounge. Besides, asking to meet in some other room often begins the preparation process for the parent.

A person once asked me in a telephone conversation if I was sitting down. I said, "Yes." He asked me if I was relaxed. I replied, "Not anymore." The questions prepared me for some news, which, in this case, happened to be good news.

Getting two parents together is becoming more and more difficult. The percentage of single-parent families or reconstituted families is high. An alternative might be to suggest to parents that they bring a friend. The impact of the news might be so traumatic that the parent stops listening after some emotionally laden words. A friend can serve as a sounding board later and may be able to give the sender of the news feedback that the parent is unable to give.

One has to be alert to how the parent is taking the news. It may be very different from what the sender had anticipated. For instance, one parent whose child was being referred for special testing was very relieved. "I was afraid you were going to tell me that he was going to be suspended from school," she said. "I knew he was having trouble, and I'm so thankful that maybe we'll get some help." The same information may be devastating to another parent. "Do you think he's crazy? What will his father say? What am I going to tell the neighbors? Why didn't you tell me he was having trouble?"

Depending upon the background and history, the same words may have entirely different meanings to different people. One person may have a concept of retardation based on a stereotype from television. Another person may have developed a concept of retardation from a visit to a state institution. A third person may actually work with mentally retarded children. To tell these three people that they have a mentally retarded child will evoke three different reactions.

One cannot assume that performance in another arena will cause a person to perform the same with his/her own child. Doctors, school teachers, and psychologists who work in the field of mental health may have the same difficulties as anyone else in hearing bad news. Even though they can intellectualize about the handicap, this does not mean that they can accept it any better than those with little experience in the field. A parent who may be able to advocate for other parents may not be able to advocate for his/her own child.

When having to deliver bad news, it is usually a good idea to set up a time for a follow-up conference. Regardless of the amount of time set aside for the initial conference, the recipient needs time to assimilate the information and prepare the questions that have to be answered.

The conveyer of bad news has to be accepting of the parent's reaction. In ancient times the messengers who brought bad news were often put to death. Parents may resent the person who has the role of informing them. They may personalize the news and want to blame the informer. A professional's skill in listening is probably crucial at these times. Giving the parents an opportunity to vent their feelings and think out loud will probably help tremendously. Being calm provides a model and a calming influence on the interaction. In this regard the teacher may want to ask the parents if they wish to be alone for a while to think and talk together privately. Taking plenty of time at this juncture will help as the situation develops in the future.

As a defense mechanism, professionals often fall back on the use of jargon. This may be unconscious, because of the comfort of talking in one's own professional language, but it does not facilitate communication between the teacher and the parent. Periodically having the parents explain what they think has been said can help the teacher determine if the message is getting across. Of course, being able to parrot the words back may mean only that the message was heard and not understood.

If diagnosticians or teachers think they may have just this one chance for interacting, they may overwhelm the parents with too much information. The amount of information a person can handle — and remember — at one time has a limit. Williams (1983) found that even when she spent considerable time with parents in test interpretation, a significant loss occurred in what they remembered or agreed upon over time.

SUMMARY

Understanding perceptions and values is basic to what this book is all about—communicating with parents. Barnlund (1976) said that, "All knowledge of the world is inescapably subjective" (p. 716). Each of us picks and chooses what bits of information we want to use from the vast amount of information available to us in our world.

That communication gaps exist between professionals and parents should come as no surprise to the sensitive teacher. These gaps occur because of the participants' differences in perception. And in a complex society even individuals who are in constant contact with each other possess distinctly different value systems. Individuals' past histories, their physical and behavioral characteristics, and the emotional feelings and values that people have may distort messages.

Understanding this is crucial for the classroom teacher, who probably has to deal with a wider range of differences than do most adults. Children come to the classroom from homes with different religions, different levels of affluence, various cultural differences, and different parental views on the importance of education. To be most effective, teachers must understand their own value systems, try to understand the value systems of the other significant adults in the child's life, and help those other adults understand their own value systems.

All of us have to deliver bad news to someone from time to time. If we are aware of the possible effects of this information on the recipients, we can work on improving our skills. Also, the physical setting and environment affect parents' ability to receive messages. The need for privacy during delivery of bad news may be vital. Further, continual "perception checking" of the parents' understanding is necessary. And one must realize that no matter how skilled one is in interpreting and presenting information, most parents will not be able to assimilate all of the data and its meaning in one session.

Finally, understanding value systems is further complicated because we as individuals do not always act on available data. Even though we are informed that smoking is harmful to our health, we continue to smoke; and while we know that obesity is potentially harmful to the heart, we continue to overeat.

A number of activities are presented in Appendix G, to help teachers review their value systems. These exercises include "Who Am I?," "The Balance Scale," "Are You a Teacher Who...," and "There Ought to be a Law." The exercises can be done individually and in most cases do not take much time. Additional activities are presented for teachers to share with parents, to help them assess and compare values. These activities are, "Are you a Parent Who...," "Whom Would You Tell?" "Handicap Ranking Scale," "Relating Domestic Values," and "Target Behavior."

Assessing one's values is a continual process. Getting to know oneself better will probably help one get to know others. As Hall (1977) said, "Understanding oneself and understanding others are closely related processes. To do one, you must start with the other, and vice versa (p. 67)."

REFERENCES

Barnlund, D.C. (1976). The mystification of meaning: Doctor-patient encounters. *Journal of Medical Education, 51.*

Curwin, R.L., & Fuhrmann, B.S. (1975). *Discovering your teaching self: Humanistic approaches to effective teaching.* Englewood Cliffs, NJ: Prentice-Hall.

Dickerson, D. (1972). *A study of the self-concepts of selected children before and after the use of the teacher-parent communication program: A behavior modification system.* Unpublished master's thesis, University of Kansas, Lawrence.

Edlund, C.V. (1969, summer). Rewards at home to promote desirable school behavior. *Teaching Exceptional Children,* pp. 121-127.

Fuller, J.M. (1971). *An evaluation of the home-school behavioral management program implemented in an intermediate classroom for the emotionally disturbed.* Unpublished doctoral dissertation, University of Kansas, Lawrence.

Geertsma, R.H., & Mackie, J.B. (1969). *Studies in self-cognition: Techniques of videotape self-observation in the behavioral sciences.* Baltimore: Williams & Wilkens.

Hall, E.T. (1977). *Beyond culture.* Garden City, NY: Anchor Books.

Korsch, B.M., & Negrete, V.F. (1972). Doctor-patient communication. *Scientific American, 227,* 66-74.

Kroth, R.L., Whelan, R.J., & Stables, J.M. (1970). Teacher application of behavior principles in home and classroom environments. *Focus on Exceptional Children, 2(3).*

Raths, L., Harmin, M., & Simon, S. (1966). *Values and teaching.* Columbus, OH: Charles E. Merrill.

Simon, S.B., & O'Rourke, R.D. (1977). *Developing values with exceptional children.* Englewood Cliffs, NJ: Prentice-Hall.

Simon, S.D., Howe, L.W., & Kirschenbaum, H. (1972). *Values clarification: A handbook of practical strategies for teachers and students.* New York: Hart.

Simonson, G. (1972). *Modification of reading comprehension scores using a home contact with parental control of reinforcers.* Unpublished master's thesis, University of Kansas, Lawrence.

Stewart, J.S. (1975, June). Clarifying values clarification: A critique. *Phi Delta Kappan,* pp. 684-688.

Vida, F., Korsch, B., & Morris, M. (1969). Gaps in doctor-patient communication. *New England Journal of Medicine, 280,* 535-540.

Williams, B. (1983). *Diagnostician-parent communication.* Unpublished doctoral dissertation, University of New Mexico, Albuquerque.

ACTIVITIES

1. Do some of the activities in Appendix G to assess your values.
2. Divide into small groups and discuss times each participant has received bad news. How was it handled? Did you hear everything?
3. Discuss the times each has had to give bad news and how it was handled. This might include things such as telling parents that their child might have to repeat a class or might need to be referred for community services.
4. Give each participant a sheet of plain paper and read the following directions to the group: "Put your paper in front of you. I'll give you some directions, and I would like you to work individually. Please don't ask any questions.

> "Starting about 2" from the top of the paper and 1" from the left side, draw a straight line about 1-1/4" long toward the bottom of the paper. Where you finished that line, start another line. Make this one about 1" long, and draw it diagonally toward the middle bottom. Start now where you finished the last line, and draw another line about 1-1/4" long diagonally toward the right middle side of your paper. Where you finish that one, start another one about 1" long toward the top of your paper. Where you finish that line, start another line 1-1/4" long diagonally toward the upper left corner of your paper. Where you finish that line, draw another one about 1-1/4" long toward the left middle of your paper. Where you finish that one, draw another line about 1-1/4" long toward the bottom middle of your paper. Where you finish that one, draw another one 1-1/4" long toward the right upper 1/3 of your paper. Now, for your last line, I want you to come back to the beginning of your last line and draw another line about 1-1/4" long toward the bottom of your paper.

> "Compare your drawing with the others in the group. Then compare your drawing with the one in Appendix G."

> Regardless of the "rightness" or "wrongness" of the directions, all drawings should have been the same since all presumably heard the same directions. Discuss why people hearing the same information draw different conclusions.

5

The Individual Conference

During his/her formative years, a child's parents and teachers are the most significant adults in the child's life. Separately and together they provide the opportunities to learn, the knowledge and skills, and the incentives needed to be a successful productive adult. With the normal child these significant adults should meet occasionally to share information about the child's progress, but with the exceptional child more frequent meetings are essential for the child's welfare. In fact, federal law, through the Education for All Handicapped Children Act of 1975 (Public Law 94-142), mandates parent-school meetings at specific points in the exceptional child's special education placement and programming process.

One of the reasons for reducing the class size for exceptional children is to give parents and teachers a chance to work together—besides the obvious reason of being able to provide the individual educational programming needed for each child. Small group meetings and individual conferences are more feasible when the teacher is able to relate to 6-15 sets of parents rather than to 30 sets of parents. Frequent interactions allow parents to share information with the teacher, receive information from the teacher, and work with the teacher in preventing and solving problems.

Conferences held before school starts in fall or early in the school year can prevent or reduce the need for problem-solving conferences. Duncan and Fitzgerald (1969) found that holding conferences at this time resulted in improved grades and attendance and reduced the number of disciplinary contacts, along with other benefits. Holding conferences early gives the teacher an opportunity to receive information from parents and to get acquainted in a nonthreatening situation.

In preparing for the initial conference, the teacher should review the available information about the child and family. Some teachers prefer not to read the cumulative records before meeting the children because they believe this knowledge will create a bias. This is unfortunate. Many times the child who has had problems in school can be identified early, and the teacher can provide assistance before the child gets enmeshed in another failure situation. The records may also include a number of inconsistencies that can be cleared up in an early conference with the parents. Another important reason for reviewing the school records is to be able to answer questions that parents may have regarding the information the school has about their child. Parents have a legal right to know what is in the school records about their child (Weintraub, 1972), and many parents do request this type of information.

CUMULATIVE RECORDS

A cumulative record folder is available to teachers on almost any child who has been in school. It contains a great deal of information, some that has been recorded and some that is inferred because of what has been omitted. The four categories of information to which the teacher should pay particular attention pertain to the child's social, academic, intellectual, and physical growth and development.

Social History

The teacher may be able to determine the family constellation from a careful reading of the records. For instance, the teacher may find out whether both parents are in the home, if both work, and whether the family includes older children. This type of information will help the teacher arrange conferences so the parents can attend and will indicate if older children might be able to help with babysitting or be available for tutoring. If no phone number is listed, communication will have to take place in person or in writing. If both parents work, arranging conferences may be difficult, and neither parent may be able to attend group meetings.

The folder may also contain some information on the child's social life—any clubs he/she belongs to and interactions with other children in the past. If problems with other youngsters are mentioned, the teacher may want to explore this with the parents in the initial conference. The teacher should be looking for techniques that can be used to help the child have some early positive experiences. Through early intervention, problems sometimes can be prevented. The parents may be able to help by providing information that will be useful to the teacher.

At this point the teacher is seeking to understand the child in his/her environment and is looking for areas to further discuss with the parents. The teacher is not trying to draw conclusions as to why the child acts as he/she does socially but, rather, to see if the child's social behavior is the same in different environments. The teacher is also trying to find out how to best conduct the forthcoming conference.

Academic Achievement

Cumulative records contain varying amounts of achievement data. The child's folder often includes achievement test scores, report cards, written reports of previous conferences, and samples of the child's work.

The information contained in the folder has probably been shared with the parents at some time in the past, although one should not assume that the parents always fully understood or remembered what was shared (Dominguez, 1982). Analysis of the data, however, may raise some questions that the teacher will want to discuss with the parents. For instance, in preparing for a conference about Billy's growth in reading as measured by the results of achievement tests (Figure 5), the teacher, Miss Skinner, noticed that in the first and second grades Billy was on grade level, but he did not seem to achieve as fast in grades three and four. She may decide to show the graph to the parent(s) during the first conference and raise the question as to what happened to Billy's progress.

Miss Skinner may also notice a rather large discrepancy between Billy's reading scores and his math scores. This may be another point to discuss. Is there any evidence of the same type of achievement patterns at home?

The parent(s) may be questioned as to the adequacy of the reporting system that has been used in the past. Parents often do not realize that

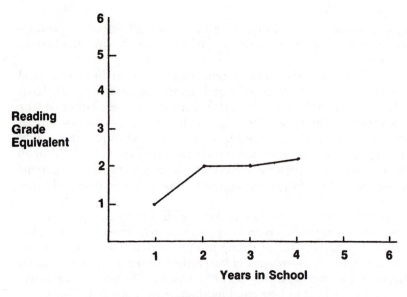

FIGURE 5
Billy's Rate of Reading Achievement

teachers can give them information about their child's progress in ways other than the quarterly report card system being used by the schools. In reviewing Billy's achievement data, Miss Skinner might feel that more frequent reporting to the parent would be beneficial to both the family and Billy.

Billy's parent may have samples of Billy's work at home that would be useful to Miss Skinner. Children sometimes do school-related tasks—such as writing poetry, keeping track of money earned on a newspaper route, drawing pictures, working crossword puzzles—that can aid the teacher's understanding of the child's ability to achieve.

Intellectual Level

Intelligence quotients (IQs) are numbers laden with emotion. Teachers and parents often attach a great deal of significance to the score and develop certain expectations that may or may not be warranted. Children with hearing losses, motor dysfunctions, emotional disturbances, and for whom English is not the primary language may have spuriously low scores. The special educator should be aware of the conditions influencing the various intelligence measures. Because of the variables that affect the testing of exceptional children, including lack of motivation, the scores obtained are more apt to reflect a low estimate than a high estimate of intelligence.

The parent may be able to provide additional information about the child that will help the teacher understand the test scores better. There is, however, a tendency for maternal overestimation of intelligence (Gorelick & Sandhu, 1967).

Physical Growth and Development

The folder may contain information on the child's physical development that will help the teacher answer some of the following questions prior to the child's entrance into class or the first conference. For Billy, Miss Skinner might ask:

1. How does his size compare to that of the other children who will be in the same room? Will the chairs be too large or too small for him? Will his height lead to nicknames that may cause fights or hurt feelings? Is he overweight? If so, will this affect his self-concept or limit his participation in recess activities?

   Teachers may forestall a number of effects of being abnormally large or small by being ready the first day of class. The effect of the size of the child is usually relative to the size of the other children in the child's social setting; however, the child functions in various environments and may have obtained nicknames before entering the special learning environment.

2. Does the child have any special sensorial defects? Routine testing by school health personnel may have indicated through vision screening that Billy has 20/200 vision. For various reasons, he may show up without glasses, perhaps because he prefers not to wear them. Miss Skinner will want to check on this during the first days of school. Similarly, the cumulative record chart may show a mild hearing loss. This should alert the teacher to provide special seating in the classroom. If this is done the first day of school, special attention need not be drawn to the child later when the teacher has to move him "because you can't hear what is going on from back there."

   Any sensorial deviations should probably be discussed with the parent in the initial conference to see what has been done and how the child feels about them. The parent may have some excellent suggestions on ways to get Billy to wear his glasses.

3. How does the child's attendance record look? Are Mondays missed most frequently? Attention to these and other questions

about the child's attendance at school is often helpful in heading off potential school problems. Obviously, if a child does not attend school regularly, the teacher's job in programming becomes more difficult. Small gains may be lost because of irregular attendance.

The critical teacher can pick up a great number of bits of information in a child's cumulative record, and this information can help prevent rough sailing at the beginning of the year. Many questions may be formulated, to be asked in initial parent conferences. If handled objectively and skillfully, these can lead to valuable insights without being considered "snoopy." The teacher and parents are both interested in the child's welfare, and most parents appreciate the fact that the teacher has taken the time to study their child in as much depth as possible prior to the first conference.

THE INITIAL PARENT CONFERENCE _____

Some school districts and day care centers permit and even encourage the teacher to have a conference with the parents before acceptance of the child into a special education program. The teacher should prepare for this conference so that it will run smoothly and be meaningful to both parties. The primary purpose of any parent-teacher conference is to facilitate the child's educational growth.

Many professionals utilize some sort of outline in initial interviews. Medical students learn to take the medical history of a patient in an organized fashion. In the initial steps of their training, a formal outline is followed fairly closely. As they become more familiar with the areas to be covered, they are able to deviate from the outline as long as they are able to cover the points at some time in the interview. Social workers use an outline for a social case study work-up. The procedure is somewhat the same, although the emphasis is more on social history than on medical history.

Educators, too, should have an outline of the information they would like to obtain in an interview (Figure 6). The outline proposed is concerned with the child's growth and development, particularly as it relates to the child's educational life (Kroth, 1972). Many of the categories in the outline are self-evident in their importance, but occasionally one forgets to explore the various areas. Appendix A illustrates this outline through four case histories.

INITIAL INTERVIEW GUIDE

A. Present Status
   1. Age
   2. Sex
   3. Grade/Class/Last year's teacher's name
B. Physical Appearance and History
   1. General impression child makes
   2. Obvious physical strengths and limitations
   3. General mannerisms, appearance, etc.
C. Educational Status
   1. Present school achievement/Kind of work/Samples of work
   2. Promotions, accelerations, retardations/Causes
   3. Relations with individual teachers, present and past
   4. Books and materials used in last educational setting
   5. Tests, individual or group/Types of measures used
D. Personal Traits
   1. Personality—general statement
   2. Attitudes toward home, friends, self, family, other students, school
   3. Hobbies, play life, leisure-time activities
   4. Educational and vocational goals
   5. Marked likes and dislikes—foods, toys, TV programs, etc.
E. Home and Family
   1. Individuals in the home
   2. Socioeconomic level
   3. Relations with home—favorite brothers/sisters, parent/other relative
   4. Regular chores, pets, etc.
   5. Home cooperation
   6. Record at social agencies
F. Work Experience
   1. Part-time jobs (summer, after school)
   2. Attitude toward work, etc.
G. Additional Information
   1. Sending school
   2. Outside agencies
   3. Private sources, doctor, mental health center, etc. (need release forms)
   4. Health information

FIGURE 6
Outline for Initial Interview

Present Status

If the teacher has no prior knowledge of the child, he/she will usually be interested in finding out the name the child likes to be called, age, and present status in school. This is a nonthreatening area with which to begin an interview. Even if the teacher has this information, he/she may want to check the accuracy of the data.

Physical Appearance

A brief observation of the child will quickly clue the teacher as to the child's more obvious physical deviations, but subtle questioning may bring out some of the less obvious characteristics—e.g., fine motor control, vision and hearing problems. In addition, many children who are handicapped have a higher than average incidence of general poor health, which could affect attendance at school. Knowledge that a child may need an operation or is highly susceptible to colds should help the teacher anticipate the coming year. If the child is taking medication, arrangements will have to be made and handled according to the existing school policy.

Educational Status

Parents should be requested to bring samples of their child's work that was sent home during the year. If the cumulative folder or the records by the past year's teacher do not contain this type of information, the parent may be able to show some examples of school-related activities.

Parents can relate some of their child's feelings about or their own experiences with the previous educational setting. Even though the experiences may be colored by isolated happenings, the teacher will be able to ascertain the parents' prevalent attitudes toward the school.

Personal Traits

An exploration of the child's hobbies, free-time activities, likes and dislikes could yield useful information for the first days of school. Books structured around the child's favorite activities may prove to be an incentive to read. Preferred activities may be used as high probability events for the completion of assignments. Hobbies can be used for "show and tell" and also may be helpful in establishing rapport with the child.

Home and Family

If the first conference is held in the home, the observant teacher may detect many characteristics of family life. Pictures, books, magazines, and newspapers reflect the family's socioeconomic status. They also indicate what references and resources the child has available for homework activities.

Determining the predominant language spoken in the home is important, and whether more than one language is used or available in the home. That the language factor has an effect on standardized testing is well known, but educators sometimes forget that it may also have an effect on home-school programs the teacher may want to set up. Written communications to the home may be misunderstood or not understood at all. Daily report cards may not be productive or may require more careful explanation when language or cultural differences occur (Edlund, 1969; Kroth, Whelan, & Stables, 1970). What may appear to be a lack of home cooperation may actually be a problem in communication.

Work Experience

With an older child, information to be elicited may include the types of jobs the child has had and whether he she is currently working. After-school or pre-school jobs may affect the child's performance at school.

Additional Information

Parents of exceptional children have often contacted or been contacted by agencies other than the school. This information does not always appear in the school records, but it is important to the teacher.

For instance, the parents may be involved in conferences that are held on a regularly scheduled basis with physical therapists, occupational therapists, psychologists, social workers, and the like. These professional specialties each have their own philosophical base, which may be confusing to the parent. It may help explain some parents' hesitancy to attend any regularly scheduled parent-teacher conference. It may also explain why the parents are reluctant to carry out certain home-school programs, in that this variety of professionals may make inordinate time and energy demands on parents without realizing the cumulative effect. Thus, the teacher can benefit from knowing who is working with the family.

Most parents want to cooperate. They are willing to work within their limits to facilitate the growth of their children. The teacher has an obligation to explore what these limits are through the study of cumulative records and skillfully conducted interviews. Understanding the demands on parents by the handicapped child, the other individuals who live in the house, and the other professionals working with the parents helps the teacher in realistic planning for the child and in *appropriate* expectations for parental cooperation.

REGULARLY SCHEDULED CONFERENCES ⸺

Regularly scheduled conferences are the "bread-and-butter" of parent-teacher interactions. They have been identified as a Level 2 need in the Mirror Model (see chapter 1) because not all parents become involved in them, even though they may be required by state and federal law and may be written into local school policy. Educators who are skilled in conferencing will be able to take advantage of these meetings to provide parents with information and also to elicit from parents information that will help with the child's education program.

The outline in Figure 7 may help the teacher prepare for a regularly scheduled conference, but nothing will replace practice under supervision. Since this activity is not usually required as part of regular teacher training programs, teachers may have to work on it after they are on the job. Videotaping oneself and reviewing the tape can be helpful.

Pre-Conference

Taking the four basic pre-conference steps listed in Figure 7 will help the conference go smoothly. First, the teacher should prepare some type of notification to be sent home. Appendix B contains Tips for Parents that can be sent home to help them prepare for this important meeting. With so little time available for the face-to-face interaction, one wants to take advantage of every minute, and the tip sheet will help. Most parents appreciate the suggestions because they convey a clear message that parents' comments are welcome. The tip sheet is writ-

CONFERENCE CHECKLIST

PRE-CONFERENCE

_____ 1. Notify
   — purpose, place, time, length of time allotted

_____ 2. Prepare
   — review child's folder
   — gather examples of work
   — prepare materials

_____ 3. Plan agenda

_____ 4. Arrange environment
   — comfortable seating
   — eliminate distractions

CONFERENCE

_____ 1. Welcome
   — establish rapport

_____ 2. State
   — purpose
   — time limitations
   — note taking
   — options for follow-up

_____ 3. Encourage
   — information sharing
   — comments
   — questions

_____ 4. Listen
   — pause once in awhile!
   — look for verbal and nonverbal cues
   — questions

_____ 5. Summarize

   (End on a positive note!)

POST-CONFERENCE

_____ 1. Review conference with child, if appropriate

_____ 2. Share information with other school personnel, if needed

_____ 3. Mark calendar for planned follow-up

Developed by the Parent Center, Albuquerque, NM

FIGURE 7
Checklist for Pre-Conference, Conference,
and Post-Conference

ten at about a sixth-grade reading level to try to ensure that most parents will be able to use it.

Preparation for the conference is the second major step. Strategies for reviewing the child's cumulative records have already been discussed. The importance of this cannot be stressed too much, because family structure changes often, and past performance compared to present performance can lead to a variety of hypotheses for "testing" in the conference.

A plan of action, or agenda, is a good idea, and it shows that the conference is considered to be important. This agenda, of course, should be flexible, with the thought that it may change after the conference starts. And teachers must remember to allow time for the *parents* to talk.

A fourth consideration is the physical environment. So much has been written on the effects of the environment on interaction that it seems like common knowledge, but horror stories are still reported frequently. Parents have reported being seated on little chairs while the teacher sits in a regular-size chair, or parents have been seated facing a light or a window. Sometimes privacy is lacking to talk over personal problems. Sometimes a table divides the teacher and the parent, or no table at all is present for writing.

Conference

Establishing rapport in a 15-minute conference is a real challenge, but it *is* important! Perhaps getting up and meeting the parent at the door with a handshake will help. A little positive anecdote or the mention of something special noticed about the child that day may break the ice—but the teacher should do *something*, not just sit there!

Guidelines for the conference should be established at the onset. If the teacher has a limited time to meet, the parents should know this. Some research on time-limited therapies suggests that people will use the time allotted to them. The climax of the information exchange tends to come near the deadline for termination. If parents do not know how much time they have, they may not raise their questions or offer comments before time to leave. Important things can take place in short time frames if the participants know what has to be accomplished and how much time has been allocated.

Taking notes during a conference is controversial. Some people think that it detracts from the personal interaction. On the other hand, many professionals (e.g., doctors, lawyers) write down the important points they want to remember. Usually, if this is explained to parents before the meeting and if the notes are shared with them at the close of the meeting, the parents do not resist. Of course, some people take tape recorders to conferences.

Parents often need encouragement to share information. Many parents have a mind-set that they are going to a meeting to hear about their child's growth and development—or lack of growth. If the tip sheet (Appendix B) mentioned earlier has been sent home, the teacher can key off the items.

Listening is discussed in chapter 3. It cannot be stressed too much, and it is often difficult for educators to do. By nature or training, educators are highly verbal people. We abhor silence and tend to speak up when silence occurs. By watching parents' body language and eye movements, however, we should be able to determine whether parents are thinking or just waiting for us to proceed.

Summarization is considered the teacher's responsibility, although the teacher might want to ask the parents to retell the most important parts of what transpired. In this way, the teacher is conducting a validity check of what transpired. During this time another conference may be scheduled and individual responsibilities delineated.

Post-Conference

Frequently the child attends the conferences. This represents a change in attitude over the past 20 years. If the student has not been present, sharing the major points of the discussion with the child is usually a good idea. The amount of information to be shared with other school personnel depends on the content of the discussion. The teacher often writes up the content of the conference, with an indication of what is to transpire between conferences. Any follow-up conference that has been scheduled should be recorded.

DEALING WITH AGGRESSION ⸺⸺⸺⸺

Occasionally one gets involved in a hostile or aggressive inter-action. This can happen with a store manager, in a teacher conference, with a child or one's mate. Usually when this happens, neither of the parties indicates a willingness to problem-solve. In this type of situation, a general feeling of helplessness is present. The tips that are included here (Figure 8) do not guarantee resolution of the conflict, but they do represent some positive steps that can be taken so as to not exacerbate the problem.

Tips for Dealing with Aggression

DO . . .

- Listen.
- Write down what they say.
- When they slow down, ask them what else is bothering them.
- Exhaust their list of complaints.
- Ask them to clarify any specific complaints that are too general.
- Show them the list and ask if it is complete.
- Ask them for suggestions for solving any of the problems they've listed.
- Write down the suggestions.
- As much as possible, mirror their body posture during this process.
- As they speak louder, speak softer.

DON'T . . .

- Argue.
- Defend or become defensive.
- Promise things you can't produce.
- Own problems that belong to others.
- Raise your voice.
- Belittle or minimize the problem.

Developed by the Parent Center, Albuquerque, NM

FIGURE 8
Tip Sheet: Dealing with Aggression

A counselor was asked to conduct a parent group consisting of parents of behaviorally disordered children. The parents came to the meeting hostile about a number of events that had occurred recently. At least that was the outward behavior. The underlying reason might have been that their children were soon to move from the comfortable elementary program to an unknown middle school program.

In opening the meeting the counselor asked for their concerns, and the parents fought for the floor. Their children didn't like the food. The kids were having to ride the bus too long. There were fights on the playground.

"Wait a minute. I'm not sure I can remember all of this," the counselor said. "Let me write it down."

She picked up a piece of chalk and went to the blackboard. Immediately the group quieted down as she began to list their concerns. She went from one complaint to another. She did not stop to discuss, argue, or defend any item. She exhausted their complaints. Then they as a group clarified those that seemed vague.

Going down the list, she elicited suggestions for solving the problems, and they made a list of things to do. The counselor tried not to own any of the problems but left them to the parents to resolve. In essence, she taught them how to approach the solutions to their own problems. She kept her voice down and didn't promise anything she couldn't produce.

When someone comes on strong, the tendency is to get defensive. A teacher may be on the receiving end of a series of problems that have nothing to do with him/her. By stopping and listening, one may let others have an opportunity to purge their feelings. Writing down the concerns slows down the tempo and assures parents that their concerns are being taken seriously. This process helps deal with heated feelings.

SUMMARY

Holding conferences with parents at the beginning of the year is important for a number of reasons. Research (Duncan & Fitzgerald, 1969) shows that early individual meetings with parents prevents or reduces problems of attendance, discipline, and dropouts and increases grades and appropriate home-school contacts. Proper preparation for an initial conference requires research on the part of teachers into the information available. A study of the student's cumulative records may raise questions for the teacher to explore with the parents.

The initial interview usually is an opportune time to establish rapport with the parents, but this cannot be done haphazardly. Working from an interview guide is consistent with many professions, such as medicine and social work. Though strict adherence to the outline is not necessary, most of the topics mentioned should be covered in order to receive valuable information from parents as an aid in understanding the child.

Regularly scheduled conferences require preparation on the part of the teacher in the same way that the initial conference does. In most school districts time restrictions are placed on the length of the conferences. To get the most out of the limited-time meeting, teachers might send home in advance some suggestions and tips on things parents can do to prepare for the meeting. At the conference, the teacher should have on hand all materials that are needed for the actual meeting. Time should be allowed for listening to the parents and encouraging them to bring up questions and comments. After the conference, major points might be shared with the child (if the child was not present) and with other school personnel, if needed.

Occasionally one gets involved in a hostile interaction. Keeping cool is essential, but it is difficult. Listening, writing down what the other person says, eliciting suggestions to resolve the concerns, not promising things one can't produce, not owning other people's problems, and not becoming defensive are ideas that work in dealing with aggression. An old adage to remember is: "If you argue with a fool, it makes two fools."

REFERENCES

Dominguez, J.C. (1982). *The effects of training on special education teachers' perceptions, knowledge and interactions with parents.* Unpublished doctoral dissertation, University of New Mexico, Albuquerque.

Duncan, L.W., & Fitzgerald, P.W. (1969). Increasing the parent-child communication through counselor-parent conferences. *Personnel & Guidance Journal,* pp. 514-517.

Edlund, C.V. (1969, summer). Rewards at home to promote desirable school behavior. *Teaching Exceptional Children,* pp. 121-127.

Gorelick, M., & Sandhu, M. (1967). Parent perception of retarded child's intelligence. *Personnel & Guidance Journal, 46*(4), 382-384.

Kroth, R. (1972). Facilitating educational progress by improving parent conferences. *Focus on Exceptional Children, 4*(7).

Kroth, R.L., Whelan, R.J., & Stables, J.M. Teacher application of behavioral principles in home and classroom environments. *Focus on Exceptional Children,* 1970, *2*(3).

Weintraub, F.J. (1972, April). Recent influences of law regarding the identification and educational placement of children. *Focus on Exceptional Children, 4*(2), 1-11.

ACTIVITIES

1. Four fictitious case studies have been prepared for role playing practice sessions (see Appendix A). A short self-test accompanies each case.

   a. The class is divided into pairs. One person assumes the role of teacher and the other the role of parent.
   b. The "parent" spends about 5 minutes reviewing the information in Case #1.
   c. The "teacher" does not look at the case but reviews the Initial Interview Guide (Figure 6).
   d. An interview of about 20 to 30 minutes is conducted.
   e. The "teacher" takes the test for Case #1.
   f. The pair discusses the interview.
   g. Roles are then reversed for Case #2.

   Discuss with the class the feelings associated with interviewing and being interviewed.

   a. Did the conference feel natural?
   b. How did the participant feel in the role of the parent?
   c. Was the "parent" allowed to talk, or was it just a question-and-answer session?

2. Discuss the reasons parents feel fearful and defensive in their meetings with school personnel. What can be done to relieve these feelings?
3. Discuss the issues of confidentiality, privileged communication, and lounge-talk as it relates to parent-teacher conferences.
4. Review a cumulative record of a child.
5. View a videotape such as *The Parent Crunch** or *Conference or Confrontation*** and discuss the interaction.
6. Videotape a real or simulated conference and review it.

The Parent Crunch may be obtained by contacting the Heart of Teaching, Agency for Instructional Television, Box A, Bloomington, IN 47401 (812)339-2203.
**Conference or Confrontation* is available from Individual and Family Development Services, Inc., 1201 S. Queen St., York, PA 17403 (717)846-2504.

6

Informational Formats for Parents

> Dad: *"What's your counselor's name?"*
> Billy: *"I don't know."*
> Dad: *"Well, who is the principal?"*
> Billy: *"I don't know."*
> Dad: *"What days do you have vacation?"*
> Billy: *"I don't know."*

Parents are interested in their children's school life and the policies and procedures that govern their educational programs. The children are not aware of some of this information, nor can they be held responsible for obtaining it.

In response to this need, many school districts, particularly the larger ones, are developing handbooks and handouts for parents, describing general policies and procedures, class schedules, a diagram of the building, calendar of events, school vacation and dismissal times, and other relevant information. To comply with state or federal (PL 94-142) legislation, parents must be informed of their rights and the rights of their children.

A real problem in some of the literature sent home, however, is that school and parent groups often do not take into account the reading levels of the parents. This is not just an issue of language preference. An analysis of various materials sent home by parent advocacy organizations and parent coalitions would lead one to the erroneous conclusion that all parents can read at the college level. Modern technology allows readability analysis of this material, on personal computers, in a matter of minutes, but developers of the handbooks and other literature rarely take advantage of this. The following selection gives an example from an actual school handout.

The educational diagnostician is a specialist knowledgeable in diagnostic and prescriptive intervention procedures. The diagnostician participates in the identification, planning, and referral of children needing special education and related services and provides consultative assistance to school personnel and parents.

Clearly, the passage is on a higher reading level than the Ann Landers column—which is a fairly good indicator of the reading level understood by most parents.

In addition to descriptions of district-wide services, special classes have policies and procedures specific to a particular population of children. The class day may be shortened, different techniques may be used by the teachers to help children control their behavior, and extra meetings may be scheduled. Parents are much more interested in the specifics of the educational program that their child is in than they are in the regular school program. Therefore, providing the parents with a handbook specific to the special program is important.

Parents of exceptional children additionally may have need for information that is specific to a situation. For instance, they may want to read books about families that have children like they have, or they may want to know what agencies in the community provide services they can use. Since not all parents need the same specialized information, including it in the general handbook is not advisable. Nevertheless, it could be made available through special handouts. Teachers can provide a real service by preparing specific handouts for parents of children in their classrooms. Also, teachers may want to encourage their school districts or individual schools to publish things such as a tutor directory and a community guide for families with exceptional children.

PREPARING A HANDBOOK ─────────────────────

Handbooks for specific classes should be short, attractive, inclusive, and written on a level the parents can understand. In general, these should not duplicate information in the general school handbook, except on topics that require emphasis. Some of the following information could be considered:

Special Personnel. This section would include the names and phone numbers of school personnel the parents may need to contact during the year—e.g., principal, teacher, counselor, nurse, school psychologist, bus driver. It might also give office hours or preferred times to call and how to make an appointment.

Classroom Procedures. Any technique that is unique to that classroom should be emphasized—the use of material rewards, study carrels, the time-out room, early dismissal time, and so on. Usually, the fewer surprises the parents have, the smoother the year passes. If any special testing or field trip request forms are different from the general school forms, these should be included.

Classroom Materials and Supplies. Special education teachers often have to call upon parents to supply special materials. A list of supplies that the parents are to provide at the beginning of and throughout the year should be brought to the parents' attention.

Transportation. Exceptional children are often bused to school. Usually this entails special rules and regulations that must be clearly pointed out to parents.

Conference and Reporting System. A section on when regularly scheduled conferences will be held and how parents can arrange for special conferences is important. If report cards are used, parents should be informed of the type of card and when they can expect to receive it.

Additional Information. Many other important pieces of information might be included, some of which depend upon the age of the child and the type of program. For instance, if the program is for secondary-age children, the parents may need to know about work-study arrangements and how children will receive high school credit. A section on tips for parents on managing child behavior might be useful if the program is for younger children. Another section might list agencies that parents can contact for special services or books that they might want to read to receive additional information. If the children use the cafeteria, the prices of lunch programs and provisions for children who bring their own lunches should be included.

Handbooks should be developed with the parents' needs in mind. Anything that all parents of children in that classroom need to know should be included. Also, special attention should be paid to how this information is to be presented. For instance, in Albuquerque some of the special education teachers have developed handbooks in both Spanish and English in keeping with the linguistic background of the parents.

DEVELOPING HANDOUTS FOR SPECIFIC SITUATIONS

The variety of handouts that could be developed for parents of exceptional children is endless. Parents appreciate receiving additional information about many specific topics and activities. Some of the topics are so common that most parents will request the information at some time. Other information is so limited that perhaps only one parent in a hundred will inquire about it.

Parents often want to know what books they can read that pertain to the handicap their child has. Some other rather common requests by parents are what games they can play with their children at home; where they can take their children on field trips; what book, record, or magazine clubs they can subscribe to; and what activities are available for their children in the summer and on trips. Since these topics are frequently requested, sections of this chapter have been devoted to discussing ways in which teachers can develop handouts giving information on this type of thing.

A number of additional topics are less frequently brought up, but teachers may want to prepare brief information sheets on things such as how to buy pets for a retarded child, helping the exceptional child with homework, clubs that a child can belong to, where exceptional children can find spare time work, preparing cookbooks for exceptional children to use, taking a child to a restaurant, and hobbies for the handicapped.

If the handout is developed by several teachers to include activities for a number of different situations, the information probably should be arranged systematically. It might be categorized by type of handicap, mental age, chronological age, the level or difficulty of the concept being presented, the readability level of the parents, or the predominant language of the parents.

Games to Play at Home

When parents and children sit down together in the evening, they can do many things besides watching television, playing computer games, or laboriously sharing a homework assignment. Many games that can be purchased in stores or made at home are fun to play. One might be critical of the claims of many of the so-called educational games, but they have the advantage of placing parents and child in an interaction situation. In addition, they may reinforce a particular skill or concept.

Categorizing games is usually difficult. For instance, the game *Anagrams* may be used for spelling. At the same time, it utilizes math skills and the ability to use abstract reasoning. The game could be listed and described under the primary skill area, with cross references to it under the other skill areas.

In a university course on counseling and conferring with parents of handicapped children, a small group of graduate students elected to prepare a handout describing games in which both parents and children could participate. In presenting the project to members of the class, they pointed out that a list of games of both a handmade and commercial nature would be endless. They also had a problem in deciding how to organize the selected games for the project.

First they felt that some information regarding how to select and play games should be shared with parents (see Figure 9). Second, they categorized the games along subject matter lines. Basically, the games were placed under the headings of mathematics, reading, and spelling. They further subdivided the categories into homemade and commercial games progressing from simple to difficult. For the homemade games they used the format below.

Name: *If I Had $10.*
Purpose: To reinforce the concept of money in a realistic world.
Materials: A sheet of paper, the daily newspaper or a catalog, and paste (can use flour and water).

Procedure:　　Give the child a piece of paper and the newspaper or catalog. Have him/her cut out (or tear out) things that are advertised for under $10. As the child selects each item, he/she must write down its name and how much it costs. Then the child must total the prices to see if he/she has spent $10. If the child spent over $10, he/she must remove an item until the total spent is $10 or just under $10.

Variations:　　The amount could be changed to $15 or to $16.45, for example. The child could also be asked to figure the taxes on each item.

In general, the format of the games was kept simple; and it was easy to see at a glance which materials were necessary to play or make the game. Variations were usually added to make a game a little more complex.

For commercial games, the same format was used to describe the game in the handout, but instructions for playing the game were kept to a minimum. Additional information included the name of the company that produced the game and the cost of the game.

Third, addresses of stores where the commercial games could be purchased locally were given. In a larger community this list allows parents from different parts of the city to select stores close to their homes. Fourth, a section of additional resources for teachers was provided. Magazines such as *Instructor* and *Teacher*, for example, were included.

Some school programs have found the "make and take" workshop to be effective. In this workshop parents are taught how to make games, nutritious snacks. Christmas presents, or other things they can take home after the meeting. This combines the activities of Levels 1, 2, and 3 of the Mirror Model. Since the use of games in teaching is well received by children, parents, and teachers alike, developing a handout on games is an excellent activity for a workshop.

Most teachers of exceptional children have a number of commercial games in their rooms to be used for various projects, learning experiences, or just free-time activities. A system could be set up so that children could check out a favorite game, just as they check out library books, except that the time limit might be for a weekend or overnight. The privilege for checking out a game could be earned by demonstrating appropriate use of the game or by other contingencies the teacher might want to use. Check-out systems need not be limited to books. Innovative teachers have set up check-out systems for pets (goldfish, gerbils, etc.), with parental permission, of course, records and pictures,

SELECTING AND PLAYING GAMES

Children need to be actively involved in the learning situation if they are to benefit from it. Games—whether purchased commercially or made at home—are good tools for getting the child involved. When choosing and playing games with children, parents and teachers should:

★ Select games that provide practice the children need and that are of interest to them. Remember—each child is an individual with unique needs.

★ Use simple games with young children. Primary children or slow learners at higher levels may find that games utilizing concrete materials (beanbags, balls, cards, etc.) are easier to learn to plan than games requiring only mental processes.

★ Teach game playing as you would teach other activities. Demonstrate as necessary. To include language practice, have children occasionally give the directions for games orally.

★ Protect children's feelings in games as in other activities. Children who are timid should not be forced to play a game against their will; perhaps giving them a game to play individually will help them feel accepted until they gain enough security to take part willingly in a group game.

★ Help children see that they must play games according to the rules. If boys and girls do have suggestions for improving the directions, do not implement the changes during a game; start over again or save the change for the next time. Emphasize that people can have permanent satisfaction as well as immediate enjoyment only if they play honestly and fairly.

★ Discuss and agree upon who is to take responsibility for putting away game materials in good order.

★ Accept only good work in games as in other activities. Let the children know this before they begin a game.

FIGURE 9
Sample Handout: Information on
Selecting and Playing Games

and so on, so it is natural that games should be included in a check-out system. Simple? Not particularly. But rewarding? Yes!

An innovative teacher of gifted children at Eugene Field Elementary school in Albuquerque developed a Parent Corner in her classroom. It was a place where parents could read and look at materials while waiting for a child. This was a nonthreatening environment, and the parent did not have to go to the city library for some books on parenting skills. Often, children and parents who did not have a great deal of reading material at home spent time together selecting books and games they could enjoy with one another at home.

Summer Programs for Exceptional Children

"What's available for my child during the summer?"

This is a common question asked of most special education teachers some time in the late spring. A prepared list of summer programs would be desirable. In fact, the teacher may want to recommend some specific programs because of the educational or social needs of individual students. Having a prepared list with the child's name at the top and certain activities starred or circled communicates to the parent that the teacher is anticipating a parental need and that he/she is taking responsibility for a year-round program.

Once the initial list has been compiled, updating it from year to year is little trouble. In fact, if the teacher maintains good relations with the office secretary or the director of special education, they will probably help by making the necessary phone calls in early spring to update the list.

Guidelines for preparing a list of summer programs are:

1. List the questions that parents will want answered. For instance:

   a. What type of handicap will the program handle?
   b. What will be the age range of the children?
   c. What is the length of program, in weeks?
   d. When will it start and finish?
   e. Is it a morning, afternoon, or all-day program?
   f. Does the program have a fee? If so, how much?
   g. Is there any provision for transportation?
   h. When and where is registration?
   i. Where will the program be located?
   j. What is the phone number to call for further information?
   k. Who is the person in charge, or who is the phone contact?

Having questions prepared in advance will facilitate the conversation with those contacted.

2. List places to contact for information about programs:

a. *Public Schools.* Someone in the administration office probably has a brochure from which one can abstract programs applicable to exceptional children.

b. *City Parks and Recreation Office.* A call to this office may not only elicit the information needed but also may provide an impetus for offering new programs for exceptional children.

c. *City Library.* Many libraries provide a variety of programs in which handicapped children can participate.

d. *Community Centers.* Larger cities have community centers that operate year-round, and many have provisions for handicapped children.

e. *Private Schools.* The yellow pages of the phone book list schools with which one may check for possible programs.

f. *Universities and Colleges.* To have practicum experiences for their students, universities sometimes set up summer school programs through the Special Education Department, Reading Department, or Physical Education Department.

g. *YMCA and YWCA.* Sports programs, arts and crafts, and the like are usually available for handicapped children.

h. *Mental Health Centers.* Some mental health centers conduct educational programs and play activities, as well as therapy sessions.

i. *Art Galleries.* Some art galleries have classes for children during the summer and will take handicapped children.

j. *Associations.* One would be remiss not to check with local associations for the retarded, children with learning disabilities, cerebral plasy, cystic fibrosis, epilepsy, multiple sclerosis, muscular dystrophy, Easter Seals, and so on. Many of these organizations collect the information desired and some sponsor programs for children.

k. *Camps.* Some camps are set up especially for handicapped children. They may be day camps or special sessions. The Y, Scouts, Easter Seals, Campfire programs, and local churches are additional sources that sometimes sponsor camps. The Council for Churches office could probably provide the information desired.

1. *Riding Academies.* Horseback riding academies sometimes have special instructive programs for physically handicapped children, as well as for other exceptionalities.

   The previous list is not exhaustive, but if one asks the persons contacted if they know of other programs, most of the programs in the community probably will be ferreted out.

3. Decide on a format for the handout.

   Since many summer programs are flexible in their definition of *handicap*, categorizing the information by exceptionality probably is not necessary. Organizing the handout by activity (educational, recreational, camping, special interests, etc.) is usually more functional. Whenever possible, one should include the information collected in response to the questions asked in Step 1.

   There are different options for presenting the information. One way would be to prepare a single booklet in which all of the information has been included. This, however, gives the parent a great deal of excess information that is not germane to specific needs. Another alternative is to describe each program on a 3" x 5" index card and file the cards in a recipe box. Updating is easy since one has to replace only a card at a time rather than redoing the whole booklet.

   A number of teachers working cooperatively to gather data on summer programs could accomplish the task in a relatively short time. This might be a workshop activity or an inservice project.

Community Services

Parents often need information on where to go to get help. Over time, professionals learn the various agencies that provide the specific services. An informal network evolves, and a telephone call may be all that is needed to get the names of persons who provide specific assistance.

In rural areas one of the important networks is the county extension program. Vonda Douglas, of the Exceptional Children Center, Utah State University, has developed a program for teaching county extension agents to be case managers for parents of handicapped children. Many materials have been developed and are available in county extension offices throughout the United States.

A Level 2 activity of the Mirror Model involves providing parents with information. Offering information about community services can be approached in a number of ways. At a basic level one may give a parent a key telephone number to call in an emergency. This number could get a parent into the network. It might be the number for the local Association of Retarded Citizens or the number of the State Director of Special Education. On another level parents may be given a directory of community services, compiled either by the city or by interested teachers. At still another level parents may be taught *how* to find the services they need rather than *what* services are available. This level of activity might lead to the development of a handout similar to the one entitled "A Parent's Guide to Community Services" (Figure 10).

Field Trips

Many handicapped children have been limited in their experiential learning because of their physical handicaps, the social mores of the communities, or reticence on the part of parents to take their children out. Another delimiting factor may be that the parents just do not know of places of interest, whom to contact about tours, and the like.

Special education teachers have realized this, and to expose children to new situations and teach them about the community have arranged field trips to the fire station, the dairy, the bakery, and so on. For the many parents who would like to do things with their children just for fun or to expand the child's horizons on weekends or during the summer, teachers could have available a handout pointing out places of interest that welcome children. Field trips also have the advantage of educating the community to the lives of handicapped children. This is an example of a Level 3 (Strengths) activity in the Mirror Model.

In compiling the handout, one might follow these steps:

1. *Brainstorm with experienced teachers.* Using the expertise of other teachers is probably the richest source of information, expecially if they are innovative and if they enjoy brainstorming. Someone will know of a nature trail for the blind, a guitar maker, an auto mechanic who enjoys children, a pet shop that children can visit with adult supervision. They also will know whom to contact for the necessary arrangements or for additional information.

2. *Ask the right questions.* As in summer programs, questions should be prepared in advance. In addition to the name of the place, the person to contact, and the telephone number, information needed includes:

A PARENT'S GUIDE TO COMMUNITY SERVICES

Associations

- Associations have handouts, and they know people.
- The Yellow Pages have a listing of "Associations."
- Associations may be similar even if not the same.

Schools

- Administrators in the public school system usually know about services available in the community.

County

- The county public health nurse or the county mental health office is available for help.

Politicians

- Voters put and keep representatives in office. Make them work for your vote.

State

- Every state has a state department of special education.

Church

- Most clergy are aware of community services and are glad to help.

Legal Services

- The Yellow Pages list free referral services if you need help.

City

- Most large cities have community resource directories.
- The United Way or the mayor's office will give referrals.

★ ★
★   **TIPS**   ★
★   ★
★   ● Keep cool!   ★
★   ● Be patient!   ★
★   ● Don't worry about hurting someone's feelings.   ★
★   ● Be optimistic! Most people want to do the right thing.   ★
★ ★

FIGURE 10
Sample Handout: A Parent's Guide to
Community Services

a. Hours open — What hours of the day are they open for visitors, and are they open on Saturdays and Sundays? Do the hours change during the summer?

b. Tours — Some places conduct tours at specified times, and they might prefer that parents and their children come at the beginning of the tour time.

c. Groups or individuals — Can parents bring their children individually or will they have to round up neighborhood children in order to have enough visitors to warrant the organization's time?

d. How does the organization feel about having handicapped children visit? Some places that parents may want to take their children have dangerous or delicate operations and may ask for specific information about the degree or type of handicap before agreeing to the visit.

e. Cost — Is there a charge for the visit? This should be checked out ahead of time to avoid any misunderstandings.

f. What might the children expect to see or do while there?

3. *Decide on a format.* The information obtained in Steps 1 and 2 should be arranged in a precise format; for example:

> Name:
> Location:
> Person to Contact:
> Phone:
> Hours:
> Days:
> Age Requirement:
> Purpose:
> Cost:
> Comments:

Once the information is compiled, it could be entered on 3" x 5" cards and filed away for later reference, or duplicated (spirit master or photocopy) on sheets and passed out to parents. The information can be organized into usable categories in a number of different ways—according to cost, age limitation, times (such as weekends, etc.), or purpose.

New teachers as well as parents will probably appreciate information on field trips. Taking children to new places is always exciting.

Collecting information in advance and preparing the children for the experience are vital, however — as most experienced teachers know.

Subscription Services

Who doesn't like to receive something through the mail — unless it is a bill? Exceptional children are no exception.

Children can receive things by mail periodically at nominal costs. A number of magazine, record, and book clubs are designed especially for children. Public libraries subscribe to a number of publications that may help parents select materials and activities for their children. *Parents' Choice* is an excellent newspaper that is published four times a year and evaluates a number of media including computer software and movies, as well as magazines, books, and records. Another source is *Periodicals for School Media Programs*, published by the American Library Association. Other sources are listed in the Resources section at the end of this chapter. Using these publications, teachers can compile a handout appropriate for parents of children in a particular classroom.

Modern technology has provided media for learning and entertainment that reach far beyond the printed word. Of course, the family must have access to the equipment necessary to use these things. Parents who might be interested in subscribing to a record/tape club, for example, can benefit from the advice of their child's teacher. First of all, the teacher can determine if listening to audio materials is a high-interest activity for the child. If given a choice of free-time activities, does the child gravitate to the record player or tape recorder? Second, can the child manipulate the equipment adequately, or can he/she learn to use it easily? If these two prerequisites are met, perhaps the parents could benefit from a handout listing some of the record/tape clubs established for children.

Information in that handout should include the name of the club, its address, and a description of the type of records and tapes the club has available. Sometimes local music stores will provide a specialized subscription service for parents upon request. *Caution*: Parents should be warned to read the contract carefully before investing in any club.

Many children have started reading or have been encouraged to read more by having subscriptions to book clubs. Something about having one's own book and starting a miniature library is gratifying to children as well as adults. Receiving books through the mail is another bonus to look forward to.

Some exceptional children who have severe reading problems or who cannot read at all will derive their greatest pleasure from receiving and owning books and having their parents read to them. Other children may have their reading skills reinforced by rereading their own books. If parents know what they have contracted for in joining a club and are satisfied with the reading level, appropriateness of illustrations, and so forth, their children will probably have a joyful experience in receiving books through the mail.

Handouts on media clubs can be compiled in workshops or as an inservice project. In preparing the handouts, teachers may want to send for the literature supplied by the subscription services and read it carefully. In the case of magazines, checking out the actual materials is desirable. In this way, one can determine for whom the activities and articles are most appropriate. The format, size, and quality of content should all be considered in the teacher's evaluation.

One might also consider compiling a list of free and inexpensive things children can send for through the mail. Some of these sources might be included in the handout to parents, and others might be used in special projects for children in class.

Travel Tips

Traveling with children, exceptional or not, can be a pleasure or an ordeal depending somewhat on planning and preparation. A handout on travel tips directed to children is usually appreciated, and it shows the concern the teacher has for the total life of the child. Once the handout is prepared, it can be used for many years since much of the information is timeless. A checklist format might be utilized. The outline for the handout might have the following major points.

1. *Easy Access Items.* One will want to keep some things handy, perhaps in a small box in the front seat. These might include a first-aid kit, snacks, litter bag, pencils, notebooks, car games or toys, and camera. The first-aid kit can be either homemade or commercial. A first-aid manual that is easy to read is also a good idea.
2. *Safety Tips.* A section on safety tips is desirable. Parents can discuss them with their children prior to the trips. Sometimes a list of safety suggestions from the child's teacher helps to reinforce the parents' "rules" ("Miss Smith says that we shouldn't throw things out of the window").
3. *Helpful Hints.* This is an area in which the teacher may want to brainstorm a number of ideas that might facilitate the trip. How

the children can be included in making plans for the trip, where to stop, how to pack suitcases to avoid confusion, and what the child can take along to play with are possibilities for inclusion. One might also suggest things for the parents to take, such as pillows, short pieces of cord, and plastic bags for dirty clothes.

4. *Games to Play.* Over the years, parents traveling with children have invented car games that make the miles fly and keep the children occupied. These games often involve the child's being able to count or knowing the alphabet. Even if the child is unable to do this, however, he/she could be a member of a team with Mom or Dad.

The games should be simple to explain. Giving the game a name and maybe writing a simple explanation of how it is played may be helpful. Some games might occur simultaneously. For instance, parents and children may decide to make a list of license plates they see from different states. Since this game may never be finished during the trip, License Poker or the Alphabet Game could be played at the same time.

As a result of his/her experience with the child, the teacher can indicate which of the items on the handout are the most appealing and appropriate for that individual child. Parents appreciate the individualization of information (which could be done with checkmarks, gold stars, highlighter, or other indicator). Since travel tips are valuable only when the family is going on a trip, this information should not necessarily be included in a handbook for all parents. It is most useful as a special-purpose handout.

Other Parent Packets

A number of other situational handouts might be developed. A group of teachers might cooperatively develop a handout on holiday suggestions for handicapped children. This could include items from some of the other handouts, such as subscriptions and commercial games, as well as toys specific to children's needs. The information would be appropriately sent out well in advance of the holiday or provided at a parent-teacher conference.

Some parents would appreciate information on "How to Have a Party for Handicapped Children." This might include what type of refreshments to serve, and when, how many children to invite or how many adults to have per number of children, games that allow a child in a wheelchair to participate (if a physically handicapped child will be attending), how long the party should last, the best time of day and week, information parents of the invited children might need, and so on.

Developing handouts represents an effort to individualize programs for parents. The handouts can be area-specific, age-specific, or general in nature. They are usually best developed in small groups, which tend to generate more ideas. In general, handouts should not be too lengthy, they should be clear, and they should include all necessary information. Teachers often find them valuable in their own teaching as well.

Examples of some of the handouts developed by the staff of the Parent Involvement Center in Albuquerque comprise Appendix B. They constitute a way of providing information, on an individualized basis, for parents and are keyed to the Mirror Model as a Level 1 activity. These tip sheets can be duplicated and sent home, passed out to parents at an open house or parent-teacher conference, included in newsletters, or made available through school, community, and business organizations.

SUMMARY

Parents need information in order to help their children have successful school experiences. Because special education programs utilize special techniques and procedures, the handbook that the public school commonly provides parents may not include the specific information that the parents of exceptional children need. Also, parents of exceptional children can profit from handouts covering specific situations. Special education teachers should think in terms of developing special handbooks and handouts that are directly relevant to parents of the children in their classes.

Handbooks should be short, attractive, and written at the parents' readability level. They should include the names and phone numbers of key personnel, any unique procedures and techniques, information on transportation, a list of special materials the child needs, and additional information germane to the population being served.

In addition to being concerned about the reading level of the material being sent home, teachers should spell and punctuate accurately any material that is sent home. Teachers and school systems are judged by their products and materials, as well as by student achievement test scores.

Situational *handouts* can be beneficial to parents if they are available when parents need them. Suggestions for homemade or commercial games that parents and children can play together are of value to many parents. The games may be used to teach academic skills or to develop cooperative social behaviors. And parents are often interested in a compilation of programs available for their children during the summer. To broaden their child's experiential environment, many parents are willing to take their children on field trips if they know where to go and whom to contact. Also, many magazine, record, and book clubs are available to provide children with hours of enjoyment. Subscriptions make good gifts. Tips on preparing for trips may be useful to parents.

The teacher can prepare any number of other specialized handouts, from knowledge of the children in his/her classroom. These projects take time to develop, but parents appreciate them, and they do contribute to their children's growth and development.

RESOURCES*

Building Blocks, a newspaper for parents and their young children, Box 31, Dundee, IL 60118.

Children's Magazine Guide, 7 N. Pinckney St., Madison, WI 53703.

Moore, N.R. (Ed.). (1983). *Free and inexpensive learning materials*. Nashville, TN: George Peabody College for Teachers/Incentives Publications Inc.

Parents' Choice. Parents' Choice Foundation, Box 185, Waban, MA 02168 ($10.00/Four issues a year).

Richardson, S. (1978). *Periodicals for school media programs*. Chicago: American Library Association.

---

*These reference materials can be found at the public library.

ACTIVITIES

1. Prepare a handbook for the parents of the children in your classroom.
2. Prepare some handouts for specific situations. Reproduce them for other teachers and for parents.
3. Generate new ideas for information sheets or handouts that might be developed for parents.
4. Do a readability analysis of the passage about the diagnostician found earlier in this chapter (page 81).
5. With a group of teachers, prepare a handbook of community services.
6. Visit your County Extension Service and review the materials it has that would be useful for parents.
7. Visit some of the community services in your area. Interview some of the staff.
8. With a group of teachers, develop a tutor directory.
9. Visit the public library and list books suitable for parents of exceptional children. Make a handout for the librarian, and ask for a parent display.

7

Reporting of Progress

Mom: The school called today.
Dad: What did he do this time?
Mom: He tore up his math paper and said he wasn't going
       to do it.
Dad: Why don't they ever call when he does his math
       instead of just when he doesn't?
Mom: They want us to come to school tomorrow morning.

Telephone calls and letters from school personnel usually strike
fear in the hearts of parents. This is because the messages are almost
always associated with some sort of unacceptable behavior on the child's
part. A mother whose child had been having problems at school once
said, "I shake every time the phone rings during the day." Many parents
wonder (as the father does in the above example) why they do not get
called when the child does something good.
   Traditionally, reports to parents have consisted of a written narrative, a report card, a conference, or a combination report card and conference about four times during the school year. The reporting periods
are "fixed" according to school policy. Most of the deviations from the

regularly scheduled report occur when a child misbehaves or when he/she is failing in school. Therefore, parents tend to associate unscheduled communications from the school with a crisis situation.

Astute observers of pupil behavior usually notice an increase in academic production just before and immediately after the date when report cards go home. At the same time, socially unacceptable behavior decreases. This is consistent with the learning theory approach (Dollar, 1972). One tends to get a surge of action around deadline times. In a sense, then, report cards do have an "effect" in that behavior changes around the date of issuance, but report cards sent home once every 9 weeks have no lasting effect for many youngsters.

REPORTING SYSTEMS

To change pupil production may mean that one will have to change the schedule of reporting to parents and also, if possible, the parents' response to the reported information. A number of studies have explored the use of daily report card systems (Dickerson, 1972; Edlund, 1969; Fuller, 1971; Kroth, Whelan, & Stables, 1970; Simonson, 1972). Essentially, all of these systems operate in a similar manner. They use a fixed interval of reporting, but the time interval has been reduced from 9 weeks or 6 weeks to 1 day. Parents receive results of the day's production at the end of every day, and they can reward growth almost immediately. Frequent reporting to parents is an attempt to provide them with the information they need for decision making, and to support the school programs. This is a Level 2 Needs activity on the Mirror Model. Usually, not all children in a class are put on the programs at the same time. The daily reporting system is reserved for those who seem to need it or who can benefit from it; however, it can be done with a class of approximately 30 children.

Daily Reporting and Merit Achievement Award System

The following program was instituted in a regular third grade class in Albuquerque, New Mexico:

> As the end of the school year approached, Sharon Schmitz decided that parental support could help maintain good social behavior in her third grade class. She believed that a weekly report would do the trick with most of the children. In early March she sent home a letter (See Figure 11).

Dear _____ :

    This note is to inform you of a new behavior report we've begun in our class. Each Friday your child will bring home a report concerning his/her behavior in school during the preceding week. This is a sample of what the report looks like:

BEHAVIOR REPORT

Name _____

Monday	Tuesday	Wednesday	Thursday	Friday
3/5	3/6	3/7	3/8	3/9

A record of my behavior this week: ★ =   ☺ =   ☹ =

                                                     Very good   OK   Bad

---

    Each day I will speak to your child about his/her behavior and mark the chart. When it is brought home on Friday, I would like your support in *praising good behavior.*

    If your child neglects to bring home the form, please ask about it. If you have any questions concerning your child's behavior, please let me know. Your part in following up on this is very important.

    Thank you for your help.

                                   Sincerely,

- - - - - - - - - - - -

    Please sign this part and send it back to school with your child tomorrow to let me know if you will support us in this effort.

FIGURE 11
Letter to Parents

Mrs. Schmitz then reproduced forms like the example in her letter so that each child had his/her own record. She used a half sheet of construction paper as a folder for the record form, and the children kept their weekly report card at their desk.

During the last 4 or 5 minutes of the day the children all placed their record forms on their desks, and Mrs. Schmitz went quietly from child to child. She had a box of stars and a felt-tipped pen, and asked each child to indicate the quality of the day with a star, a smiling face, or a frowning face. Usually the children were able to assess their performance fairly accurately. At the end of the week the children took their records home.

The results of the program seemed to justify the time spent. Mrs. Schmitz said, "This report was intended to reward good behavior and alert the parents to any current behavioral problems. The response by parents and children was favorable. Parental support, recognition from the teacher, and personal satisfaction worked in concert to reinforce positive behavior."

In addition to a weekly report being sent home, the program had a number of positive features. First, it was an event that settled the class down at the end of the day. All the children sat quietly in their seats for this final event of the school day. Second, each child had a mini-conference with the teacher every day. Some children may go through a day with little, if any, recognition by the teacher because of the many demands on the teacher's time. Third, the parents were involved in the program. They were alerted to the system, and they could reinforce the child for school performance more often than once every 9 weeks.

Another reporting technique that Mrs. Schmitz used effectively was the Merit Achievement Award System. This program was planned so that every time the child accomplished the designated behavioral objective, a certificate was filled out and sent home. The teacher designed the certificates and made copies for each of the children (Figure 12). According to her, "The children valued and respected these awards. The first certificate was used to stimulate children as they acquired the skill of cursive writing. Later they helped decide which other skills were important enough to be rewarded with a certificate."

In the past, Mrs. Schmitz had called or sent notes home when she felt she needed parental assistance with children who were having problems socially or academically. She developed the two programs described to give parents information of a more positive nature. All the children in her room had "good" or "excellent" social behavior in her classroom most of the time. Through the weekly report card system, she was able to provide the parents with this information. By setting aside the last 5 minutes of the school day for the activity, the system guaranteed that every child would receive her attention every day and

```
┌──────────────────────────────────────────────┐
│                  CERTIFICATE                   │
│                                                │
│  This will certify that _____ │
│  has learned to write all the letters in the   │
│  alphabet in cursive writing. This skill is a  │
│  valuable tool for good communication.         │
│                                                │
│  _____   │
│                    (teacher's signature)       │
│                                                │
│              _____       │
│                         (date)                 │
│                                                │
│  School Name _____           │
│                                                │
│  Class _____                         │
└──────────────────────────────────────────────┘
```

FIGURE 12
Merit Achievement Award System: Certificate

also gave her an opportunity to systematically reinforce the children for appropriate social behavior.

The Merit Achievement Award System offered a means whereby *every* child received recognition for academic performance. A large percentage of children in the public school system proceeds through the various grades without ever obtaining any symbols of accomplishment while just a few children receive many certificates, medals, trophies, and other mementos. The Merit Achievement Award System used by Mrs. Schmitz was based on the behavioral objectives that she had established for each child in her class, thus ensuring that all children could obtain recognition. It also provided parents with the knowledge that their children were progressing. Providing parents with positive reports when they are indicated helps set the tone of a positive school environment for children. It also reassures parents that teachers can see positive behavior as well as negative behavior.

Daily or weekly reporting systems work with secondary students as well as with elementary children. Lea Long, a secondary teacher in Albuquerque reported, ". . . my students are getting weekly report cards this year . . . . I don't require that they take them home, but some parents are asking for them each Friday. Even with the others, I believe I'm seeing an effect. Secondary BD kids pretend they don't really care, but they ask for them—one demands his early on Friday morning, then tears it up to make sure everyone knows it's not important. But he looks at it, and even checks it!"

Teacher-Parent Communication Program

A Teacher-Parent Communication Program was used by Dickerson (1972), Fuller (1971), and Simonson (1972) to facilitate child growth in the classroom. A workshop to explain and instruct teachers in using the program has been developed by the SEIMC, Lawrence, Kansas; and it has been used with numerous groups of teachers.

The program is somewhat more complex in design than the programs used by Mrs. Schmitz. As a result, the Teacher-Parent Communication Program is usually used with a single child in a regular class who has been identified as needing special attention, or with a small number of children in a self-contained class for exceptional children if it is fully implemented. The program can be modified to use with a child in a single subject. The procedure is as follows:

1. When a child has been identified as having a social or academic problem in the classroom and has not responded to typical behavior modification programs or remedial techniques, a conference with both parents, the child, and the teacher is held.
2. The problem is delineated, and a home-school program is developed individually for the child.
3. A worksheet is completed. This becomes, in essence, a behavioral contract. The academic level of performance needed to receive an "acceptable" card is specified, along with the social behavior desired. The number of cards to be required daily is listed; this usually consists of 10 cards, one given to the child every 40 minutes. The number of "acceptable" cards that will entitle the child to a daily reward and the possibility of a weekly reward is agreed upon.
4. Each card has a place for four checkmarks. The teacher checks either "acceptable" or "unacceptable" for academics and either "acceptable" or "unacceptable" for social behavior.
5. The parents and child agree upon the rewards to be earned. The daily rewards are usually simple—stay up an extra 15 minutes, watch a favorite TV program, etc.

Consistency in carrying out the program is stressed for both the parents and the teacher.

This program is interesting in that the child is involved in the conference, and he/she has a say in the rewards. Also, the child is able to listen to the agreements made so that no misunderstandings should arise later.

Research by Dickerson (1972), Fuller (1971), and Simonson (1972) would indicate that the program is effective. The investigators stressed, however, that consistency is of utmost importance and that unrealistic expectancies should not be demanded. The student who is in the program should not be expected to behave better than other children in the same class.

The benefits of the program are many. As social and academic behaviors change, parents are not only kept informed but their help is solicited as well; the parents are able and encouraged to give positive reinforcement frequently; and the children are able to see the relationship between their behavior and its consequences.

Edlund Program

The program described by Edlund(1969) has many features in common with the Teacher-Parent Communication Program. In the checklist system employed, the child was given checkmarks for successful completion of academic work and acceptable social behavior. Programs were individually developed, depending upon the past performance of each child.

A series of conferences was held with parents, either individually or in groups, to explain the checklist and the principles of reinforcement the parents were to employ. Edlund pointed out a need for weekly contacts, either in person or by phone, for a substantial period of time, to answer questions and ensure that the program is being followed.

Parents selected the rewards to be used. They were encouraged to observe their children at home to determine the things or events that would be reinforcing to the child. Usually the amount or quantity of reward per checkmark was discussed in the conference sessions to try to assure that the children did not receive too much or too little for their efforts.

The program also covered procedures for phasing out the reward system, problems associated with the child's failure to bring the checklist home, the techniques employed to discourage forgery of checkmarks, and possible parental resistance. These are common problems associated with the use of daily report systems. They are not insurmountable, but people *will* try to beat the system, and even with programs that have proven to be successful, some parents are extremely reluctant to participate.

Edlund suggested that having parents meet in *groups* helps to reduce resistance to the program. Parents can often answer other parents in meaningful ways. Their testimonials tend to stimulate and reinforce each other.

Kroth, Whelan, and Stables' Project

Parents were used to reinforce their children's academic and social behavior in a class of emotionally disturbed junior high school pupils (Kroth, Whelan, & Stables, 1970). Children in the program were being educated in a structured environment that utilized behavioral principles. Donations of trading stamps by a local service organization had been used in a token economy system to facilitate pupil growth. When the trading stamps were no longer available, parents were asked to become involved in the reinforcement process. A simple daily report card was developed listing the subjects in which the child was enrolled, plus social behavior (Figure 13). For the academic subjects being taught, scores were recorded on the card as the percentage of problems worked correctly; the social behavior was reported either on a 1 to 10 scale or as a percentage score. The percentages were added and divided by the number of subjects being measured, to obtain a daily average. Each child filled in his/her own report card. Then the teacher checked, dated, and signed it.

The system was discussed in a parent group meeting. Upon its acceptance by the parents, it was implemented. Parents were instructed in graphing procedures and in methods for applying rewards for growth. They were encouraged to utilize rewards that were within their individual value systems. The emphasis was on using a reward system rather than punishment procedures. The project directors reinforced the parents with praise at the regularly scheduled conference.

To test the effects of the program, parents were encouraged to select two or three specific areas of the report card on which to concentrate their reinforcement efforts and to withhold knowledge of those areas from the staff for a few months. In the areas that the parents chose to selectively reinforce, the children grew more than they did in the areas that the parents did not reinforce, suggesting that this is a viable procedure for changing child behavior. Parents can greatly influence what happens in the classroom if they are invited to participate in the program.

DAILY REPORT CARD

Name _____

Language Arts	_____
Mathematics	_____
Science	_____
P.E.	_____
Literature or Reading	_____
Spelling	_____
Typing	_____
Social Behavior	_____

Total Points Daily _____ Daily Average _____

_____	_____
Date	Teacher's Signature

FIGURE 13
Kroth, Whelan, and Stables' Project:
Daily Report Card

Other Reporting Programs

The use of daily or weekly report card systems as described in the preceding sections is not new to teachers. Many teachers have called parents or sent letters home when children have performed appropriately. But they probably have not systematized their efforts in quite the same ways as the programs outlined above, and usually little attempt has been made to evaluate the results in ways other than a subjective report indicating that it did or did not have a particular effect.

Teachers are experimenting with a number of other ideas that sound like potent ways of sharing information with parents. Some of the ideas could be measured as to their change effect, while for others it may be rather difficult.

Judy Zimmer, Minot, North Dakota, has used the camera to record children in action. A picture catching a child while he/she is working can be used to show parents examples of the child in the educational environment. It can also be used with the child as an example of the type of behavior the teacher would like to have him/her model. Happy children, smiling and cooperating, are good "reports" to share with parents. If the camera is used to record only examples of poor behavior, it could tend to reinforce "clowning" or deviant behavior.

Jeanne Marie Stables has had junior high school level children write notes to their parents telling of their academic progress. These letters are written just before a parent conference and held until the parents come to talk with the teacher and look over their children's work. The parents then are asked to respond to the child's letter with one of their own that will reinforce the child's growth.

Ann Tice, of Shawnee Mission, Kansas, has used the tape recorder in a similar way. When the parents come for a conference, they are asked to look over their child's work and then record a message on the tape recorder, commenting on some of the good work they observed. The following morning the children listen to their parents' messages. The recordings can be saved as a permanent record for future reference.

Jerry Chaffin, University of Kansas, has discussed the possibilities of combining Super-X movies with tape recordings as reports to parents. In this way, parents can observe their children in selected samples of educational activities and listen to their children read and perform other educational tasks. Not only would this provide parents a permanent record of their children's growth, but it would also enable teachers to review the tapes—much as a coach reviews game films—to ascertain strengths and weaknesses in children's performance.

Carrie Gymes, elementary BD teacher in Albuquerque, has found an effective application for videotape. She uses it as an incentive for attendance at her parent group meetings. It captures children's progress in social behavior and also is used to illustrate projects being carried out in the classroom.

Bill Heward and Tim Heron, professors from Ohio State University, have demonstrated the potential of using a telephone answering service to improve communication between home and school. By putting homework assignments on a telephone answering device, they were able to heighten children's performance. They also offered the answering service to teachers for announcements and reminders to parents, with assigned times for each teacher to use the service. This reduced the number of excuses that "my child forgot to bring the notice home."

Currently, a couple of home reporting systems are available on computer disks. The ease of computer-managed data aggregation and reporting should make daily and weekly reporting so simple that the major issue will not be one of "I don't have time" but, rather, one of not believing in the practice from a philosophical base.

Modern technology and media have enabled better reporting to parents in a variety of ways. Videotapes, cameras, movies, tape recorders, and computers, as well as traditional verbal and written records, have widened the avenues for more accurate reporting. We are limited only by our imaginations.

Usually a good rule of thumb in using these alternative reporting systems is to try to show examples of what children can do rather than to point up their deficits. This is particularly true with children who have been classified in some way as *exceptional*. All too often their weaknesses have been highlighted. There is a need to record and reinforce their successes.

SUMMARY

In most public school systems, report cards and parent-teacher conferences are on a quarterly basis. The report usually consists of a summary of the child's work for a 9-week period. A quarterly report may be adequate for many children and their parents, but the reports are so far apart that some children do not receive the reinforcement they need for academic and social growth. If the teacher expects the parents to reinforce academic growth, the parents must have information from the school more often. This may consist of a weekly or daily report card or spontaneous reports of good academic or social growth.

A number of studies that have been conducted show the positive effects of daily report card systems (Dickerson, 1972; Edlund, 1969; Fuller, 1971; Kroth, Whelan, & Stables, 1970; Simonson, 1972). All children in a class are seldom put on a daily report card system at the same time, but it can be done.

Teachers have developed a number of different systems to report information to parents. Taking pictures of children at work and play, having children write notes, letting parents or children tape record messages to each other, and using videotape are just some of the possible ways of reporting to parents. There are many viable options for sharing information with parents more frequently than the traditional quarterly report card.

REFERENCES

Dickerson, D. (1972). *A study of the self-concepts of selected children before and after the use of the teacher-parent communication program: A behavior modification system.* Unpublished master's thesis, University of Kansas, Lawrence.

Dollar, B. (1972). *Humanizing classroom discipline—A behavioral approach.* New York: Harper & Row.

Edlund, C.V. (1969). Rewards at home to promote desirable school behavior. *Teaching Exceptional Children, 1*(4), 121-127.

Fuller, J.M. (1971). *An evaluation of the home-school behavioral management program implemented in an intermediate classroom for the emotionally disturbed.* Unpublished doctoral dissertation, University of Kansas, Lawrence.

Kroth, R.L., Whelan, R.J., & Stables, J.M. (1970). Teacher application of behavior principles in home and classroom environments. *Focus on Exceptional Children, 2*(3).

Simonson, G. (1972). *Modification of reading comprehension scores using a home contract with parental control of reinforcers.* Unpublished master's thesis, University of Kansas, Lawrence.

ACTIVITIES

1. Develop a short report card to be used for daily or weekly reporting to parents.

2. Set up a program for a child or a few children using special reporting techniques; record changes that have occurred in either academic or social behavior because of the program.

3. Call different parents every day for a month, and tell them something good that their child did that day. Try to call the parents of each child in your classroom at least once during the month.

4. Take a picture of a child in your class (particularly one who is having academic problems) working on something and send it home to his/her parents.

5. Make some different kinds of certificates or awards to send home when a child accomplishes a behavioral objective in your room.

6. To counteract each "bad" note you have to send home to a parent, send a "good" note to the parent of another child who has done something well.

8

Parent Group Meetings

Some topics are not of interest to all participants of regularly scheduled PTA meetings for the whole school. They are also topics that are not best raised during individual conferences, because that would consume too much time. They are, however, relevant topics for all members of a special interest group. One of the quickest ways of presenting this type of information to parents is the small group meeting. The small group meeting should not be confused with small group sessions designed to train parents in specific child rearing techniques or meetings whose goal is a therapeutic outcome. The major purpose of the small group meeting that is the subject of this chapter is to relay information to parents effectively and efficiently.

Parent group meetings can be viewed as either a Level 2 or 3 activity in the Mirror Model, depending on the intensity of the information being shared. If the meeting projects a one-way flow of information without much training, it is a Level 2 activity. If it involves training over time, it would more likely be regarded as a Level 3 activity.

PLANNING BY PROFESSIONALS _____

Before the school year begins, the teacher should decide what group meetings will be necessary during the year and the purposes they are to fulfill. The next thing to be considered is when these meetings should occur to have maximum meaning to parents. The teacher has to decide who will be involved and the best format by which to relay the information. Each special education program will dictate the content and type of meeting. The following topics are some suggestions.

1. *Classroom Policies, Procedures, and Techniques.* Early in the school year the teacher would be wise to meet with parents whose children are in special education programs, to explain the policies and procedures he/she uses. Additional participants in the program might be the bus driver and the principal.

   Transportation is often worrisome, and the sooner parents understand the rules and the reasoning behind them, the better it is for both school and home. If the special education program has early dismissal, the reason for this should be explained to parents. Some teachers use special techniques in their classrooms, such as reward systems and time-out rooms. How and why they are used should be brought up. If children are in special classes for part of the day and regular classes for part of the day, this procedure should be explained.

   The meeting might be held in the teacher's classroom so parents can see and perhaps use the special equipment that the teacher has available. The parents should be encouraged to ask questions. Expectations on the part of both teacher and parents can be discussed and clarified. Name tags should be used so that parents and teachers can identify each other by name early in the year.

2. *Grading Procedures.* Before the first grading period, the teacher should explain the method he/she will be using to evaluate children and report to the parents. Parents will be interested in deviations from the normal reporting procedures and how these deviations will affect the child if he/she is returned to the regular classroom.

   If conferences are to be held for the purpose of reporting, parents can be informed of what to expect in the conference and how they can prepare for the interview. Since conferences are considered a vital activity and are mandated under the Education for All Handicapped Children Act, providing parents with additional information, such as the tips listed in Figure 14 (and

PARENT TIPS FOR SCHOOL CONFERENCES

A parent-teacher conference offers a chance for two important adults to talk about how a child is doing in school. It is a time for you, as a parent, to bring up concerns you may have about your child's progress. Since the time allowed for conferences is often limited, both parents and teachers can benefit from planning ahead.

Here is a checklist that may help you get ready for your conference.

HOW TO GET READY

_____ 1. Make a list of questions and concerns.

_____ 2. Ask your child if he/she has questions for the teacher.

_____ 3. Arrange for a babysitter for small children.

QUESTIONS YOU MAY WANT TO ASK

_____ 1. In which subjects does my child do well? Is my child having any trouble?

_____ 2. Does my child get along with other children?

_____ 3. Does my child obey the teacher?

_____ 4. How can I help at home?

QUESTIONS THE TEACHER MAY ASK YOU

_____ 1. What does your child like best about school?

_____ 2. What does your child do after school? (What are his/her interests?)

_____ 3. Does your child have time and space set aside for homework?

_____ 4. How is your child's health?

_____ 5. Are there any problems that may affect your child's learning?

_____ 6. What type of discipline works well at home?

AT THE CONFERENCE

_____ 1. Please arrive on time.

_____ 2. Discuss your questions and concerns. (Use your checklist.)

_____ 3. Share information that will help the teacher know your child better.

_____ 4. Take notes if you wish.

AFTER THE CONFERENCE

_____ 1. If you have more questions or you ran out of time, make another appointment.

_____ 2. Tell your child about the conference.

_____ 3. Plan to keep in touch with the teacher.

_____ 4. If you were satisfied with the conference, write a note to the teacher.

FIGURE 14
Handout: Parent Tips for School Conferences

Appendix B), can be helpful. A number of teachers in the Albuquerque Public School System send copies of this tip sheet home before conferences, and this information is also discussed at parent group meetings.

Counselors, school psychologists, and teachers may be the major presenters. Any special testing that will be done during the year could be reported at this meeting. Time should be allowed for discussion. Parents may want to bring up issues regarding the whole school system's grading policy, but the focus should be kept on the special education programs.

3. *Active Participation.* Most educators do not want parents to be passive in staff meetings or conferences. As a result, parent meetings have been held to teach parents to be active participants in the educational process. These workshops have been conducted in elementary, mid school, and high school groups. An outline of the major points "On Being an Active Participant" can be found in Appendix B, and the procedure has been discussed by Kroth (1979).

4. *Introduction of Specialists.* As the year progresses, the teacher may want to introduce the specialists who support the special education program in some way. The purpose of this meeting may be twofold: to provide parents with information regarding who is available for assistance to the teacher, parents, and children; and to give the supporting personnel recognition for their work.

Because of the number of persons who could be involved, the teacher may want to hold two or three different meetings. One meeting might include the speech therapist, nurse, counselor, and school psychologist. They often do special evaluations, such as intelligence and achievement testing, hearing and vision screening, and speech assessment. They can explain their instruments and how the results of their testing will be used. Another meeting might include the physical education teacher, librarian, and cafeteria personnel. These individuals can give parents a demonstration and a tour of the facilities of which they are in charge, and explain how they relate to the special education program.

5. *Related Outside Agencies.* Some special education programs rely heavily on outside agencies. Personnel from agencies such as guidance centers, mental health centers, and family service centers might provide direct support to children and their families. For older youth they might provide job placement services.

If business men and women in the community are actively hiring exceptional children and working closely with the schools, they are good prospects for speaking to parent groups. Both parties stand to benefit from the exchange. The business representatives could explain the criteria they use in selecting applicants to work for them, and they could give parents suggestions on things to do at home to improve their child's chances for employment.

6. *Seminars.* Over the past 5 years, the staff of the Parent Involvement Center in Albuquerque has experimented with a variety of parent meetings in a number of different settings. Featuring guest speakers on topics such as assertive discipline, adolescence, drugs, divorce, communication skills, and understanding your handicapped child has generated high interest among parents. At one mini-conference for parents on a Saturday, over 700 parents attended. Sponsoring workshops for parents in industry during their "brown bag" lunches has been well received by both industry and parents. Offering these meetings to large groups of parents assures better attendance. It also responds to the time constraints of working parents.

7. *Television and Radio.* Other avenues to explore are television and radio. Public-access channels may be a vehicle for presenting information to parents who cannot attend meetings in person. Some TV stations feature public information programs in their formats, including ideas from educators. The radio is an even more accessible media form for parent educators, and well planned programs are welcomed. Denny Edge, of the University of Louisville, developed a series of 1-minute informational spots for radio, as just one example.

The teacher may want to have meetings on any number of other topics. One should remember, however, that the meeting should always have a purpose.

PLANNING BY PARENTS

Parents, too, have ideas for meetings. The teacher should establish a small advisory committee of parents to help plan some meetings. This same advisory group can serve to improve attendance at the meetings.

In selecting members of this advisory group, the teacher should look for parents who have a variety of interests and those who will be willing to serve for a year. They should be representative of the total group, if possible. In general, they should not be expected to set up more than one or two meetings for the year. Activities of the advisory group might include:

1. *Surveying the Group.* Either by questionnaire or by personal contact, the advisory group should survey the other parents to find out what topics (ones that are not already planned) they would like to see covered. They may keep the questionnaire open-ended, or they may suggest a list of topics from which to choose. Examples of surveys are given in Appendix C.

2. *Arranging for Participants.* If the parents have decided they would like to hear from a state legislator or the school superintendent, members of the advisory group should make the contact, arrange for dates, and complete other details. It is their request and their program, and this should be clear.

3. *Conducting the Meeting.* The advisory group should choose a spokesperson to introduce the speaker and to make necessary arrangements for special equipment or materials. Refreshments and provisions for location of the meeting are additional considerations.

In the meetings that parents plan and conduct, the teacher should stay in the background. Utilizing parents' *strengths* in this manner is an example of a Level 3 activity in the Mirror Model. The teacher may be called upon to offer advice and help with arrangements, but he/she should keep a low profile. The parents should get the credit for the meeting, and they should take the responsibility for it.

Although attendance at and attitudes toward PTA and PTO meetings have fluctuated over the past decade, the idea of bringing parents together for meetings is still viable. Unfortunately, attendance figures often have been used as a measure of success. Perhaps a more basic barometer relates to the match between the parents in attendance and the content of the meeting. Meetings should not be held for the sole purpose of having a meeting.

SUGGESTIONS FOR IMPROVING MEETINGS

A number of things can be done to enhance the probability of making informative programs successful.

1. Initiate a parent telephone calling tree, in which parents call other parents to remind them of the meeting.
2. Keep the business part of the meeting short. Is the information presented during this segment necessary or important for all the parents in attendance? If not, delete the expendable information.
3. Don't overtalk or line up more presenters than can be comfortably handled in the amount of time allocated for the meeting.
4. Start on time. Everyone's time is important. To keep attendees waiting is discourteous.
5. End on time. Let the parents know ahead of time when the meeting will be over, and stick to it. Many parents have had to get babysitters or have other commitments after the meeting.
6. Provide an activity room or area for children. Parents are more apt to come to a meeting if provisions have been made for their children. The high school Future Teacher's Association is one possibility for contact to supervise the activity room. Consider setting up television or cartoon movies. Maybe even have refreshments for the children.
7. Provide refreshments for the parents, possibly even while the program is going on. Often cookies and coffee are left over after the meeting because some of the parents have had to get home and put their children to bed. Having a cup of coffee or punch and a cigarette during the meeting may help put parents at ease.
8. Occasionally have the students perform. Parents like to see their children do things. A variety show, physical education activities, a song or two, a display of pupils' art, or a videotape of a classroom activity is an added incentive for parents to come to a meeting.
9. Allow a question/answer time, and even plant a question or two in the audience to get the ball rolling. The teacher might sit among the parents during the presentations and ask an early question.
10. Provide paper and pencils for the parents. Parents seldom think to take paper to a presentation. Parents might take notes on important ideas that come up. Otherwise they can just doodle.
11. On occasion take some pictures of the parents. Regardless of what people say, most people like to have their pictures taken. Show the children these pictures so they can see that their parents come to school, too.
12. Jot a note to parents thanking them for coming. Solicit a parent to help with this, thereby taking advantage of parent strengths.

At least part of the reason for declining attendance at and waning enthusiasm for the PTA-type parent program has been associated with the attitude that meetings must be held monthly and that they should be of broad general interest, involving parents from the whole school. In contrast, if parents who have a common bond — e.g., band members' parents, athletes' parents, parents of handicapped children — are brought together and the program is specific to that audience, attendance will probably increase. Also, most speakers prefer to address special interest groups.

FORMATS FOR SPECIAL EDUCATION MEETINGS

Special educators in Odessa, Texas, have developed a number of different means of presenting information to parents. Two types of programs that fit into the PTA approach and that demonstrate unique ways of presenting information to parents are the *slide/tape presentation* and the *dialogue technique.*

To illustrate the Odessa work-study program to parents (and also for use with community groups), a narrative describing various aspects of the program was written and taped. Slide pictures were taken to depict the story. These were used together in meetings with parents whose children were eligible for the program and with service groups that might be interested in participating in the program. This was a good public relations technique because many business people in the community were involved; and showing slides of children at work in different businesses was a way of rewarding those who had participated.

The dialogue technique is clever in that parents can often relate to the characters in the dialogue. In this case, the dialogue was between a mother and her child after school. It gave the professionals in Odessa a vehicle for explaining what a child in a special program meant when he said he had been playing games all day in school. The dialogue raised a number of questions in the mother's mind as to what was going on in the special class, and the answers helped explain some of the "games" and activities. In the meeting, some of the games were demonstrated. A second brief dialogue was presented in which the child stated what he did at school, but now the mother understood: "That must be to develop eye-hand coordination or to encourage cooperative play behavior." The dialogue technique provides an avenue of communication that lets the parent know that school personnel understand possible misinterpretations. It is a good instructional device, and also fun.

SUMMARY

The earlier discussion in chapter 1 pointed out that parents do not always have the time, strength, energy, and interest to attend all of the events the school provides. Families have many priorities. Sometimes parents might be better off being at home with their children than attending a meeting of low interest or relevance to them. In other cases, the parents may be trying to take care of the basic needs of keeping food on the table and clean clothes on the child.

One efficient way of providing a number of parents with some specific information is through a series of small group meetings. These should be well thought out and carefully planned as to purpose, place, and participants. They should also be timely. A number of topics—such as classroom policies, grading procedures, and the introduction of supporting personnel—are relevant to most special education programs.

Parents should also have an opportunity to plan a meeting or two a year around topics in which they are interested. The parents should have the responsibility for surveying the group for topics, making arrangements for speakers, rooms, refreshments, and conducting the meeting.

Teachers and parents can do a number of things to improve the chances for success of a series of meetings. Keeping the meeting short and on target, starting and ending on time, and having some provisions for children during the meeting are all appreciated by parents.

An interesting format for explaining parts of the program to parents is beneficial. Special educators in Odessa, Texas, have used slide/tape presentations and a dialogue technique to move away from the more formal presentation style often found in the PTA-type program. We need to plan as carefully for parents as we do for children.

REFERENCES

Kroth, R.L. (1979). Unsuccessful conferencing (or we've got to stop meeting like this). *Counseling & Human Development, 11*(9), 1-11.

ACTIVITIES

1. Plan a series of short information-type meetings for parents. Put down the purpose of each meeting, who would present the information, and when the meetings would be held during the year. Justify your choice of meetings.

2. Develop a slide/tape presentation or a dialogue presentation to be used in a parent group meeting.

3. Survey parents to find out topics on which they would like to have information. Develop a questionnaire or interest inventory for this purpose. (Appendix C provides some sample surveys.)

4. Invite a group of parents of exceptional children to form a panel to discuss parent meetings. Ask them to react to issues of the importance of such meetings, weaknesses of the meetings, hardships on the parents to attend the meetings, and suggestions for improving meetings.

9

Defining the Problem

"Mrs. Smith?"
"Yes."
*"This is Miss Rogers, Johnny's teacher. I'm having a little
problem getting Johnny to work on his spelling. Do you
suppose you could help me?"*
"I don't know much about teaching spelling. . ."
*"But you do know Johnny, and I could use your help if you
could spare a little time."*
"I'll stop in after school when I come to pick up the kids."

The techniques and procedures described in Sections I and II are
primarily means for information sharing between parents and teachers.
Utilizing many of these practices can prevent problems from arising or
make the solution of identified problems easier. In addition, some of the
techniques discussed in chapter 3, "Listening to Parents," and chapter
7, "Reporting of Progress," could be considered as problem solving
techniques. If parents and teachers have established a good working
relationship, problem solving becomes a cooperative venture.

In the conversation at the beginning of this chapter, Miss Rogers and Mrs. Smith are setting the stage for a problem solving conference. Miss Rogers has a problem in that she is having trouble getting Johnny to work on his spelling. She is soliciting help from Mrs. Smith, Johnny's mother. At this point she is not blaming Johnny for not doing his spelling, nor is she blaming Mrs. Smith. She is accepting responsibility for the problem. She has made an initial attempt to define the problem as "working on spelling."

Problem solving has two rather important initial steps. The first is to determine ownership of the problem. Though the answer to the question of "who has the problem" would seem likely to be self-evident, it is not always that apparent (Gordon, 1970). A problem is often like the proverbial "hot potato." Nobody wants to take hold of it. In the above example, if Miss Rogers were less self-confident in her role as teacher, she might have claimed that Johnny had a problem or that Mrs. Smith had a problem rather than taking the responsibility herself. So a first step is to analyze where the problem lies and, therefore, who is going to have to take the major responsibility for its solution.

The second step is to define the problem in operational terms and identify the situations in which the problematic behavior occurs (Bersoff & Grieger, 1971; Krumboltz & Thoresen, 1969). Initially, problems are often stated in general, global, nondefinitive terms. For instance, if Miss Smith had said that Johnny was irresponsible, the label "irresponsible" would have to be redefined in more definitive terms.

The listening techniques described in chapter 3 are particularly helpful toward accomplishing these first steps. The person using the listening techniques, however, must realize what he/she is trying to accomplish—i.e., determination of ownership of the problem and an operational definition of the behavior that is considered to be a problem.

WHOSE PROBLEM IS IT? _____

A counselor once said, "The person who comes to me is the one who has the problem." That statement is probably a good observation regarding the question of who owns the problem. Often we look at how a problem is presented rather than who presents it. Analyze the following statements:

Mother: "*Your son didn't get in until 12 o'clock last night.*"

First, the mother is trying to push ownership of the problem onto the father by saying "your son." Second, the implication is that the son has a problem of not getting home on time. In reality, the mother is the one who is concerned, and she has the problem of dealing with the son who gets home late. The boy was probably enjoying himself immensely; therefore, he does not view his behavior as a problem. The father may not have considered it as a problem until the mother said "your son." The mother and the father could well end up arguing about whose problem it is, and little will be done to improve the mother's ability to solve her problem of dealing with a son coming home late.

Teacher: "Your son would rather draw than do his math."

Does the boy have a problem? No, he is probably quite content while drawing; and he finds this activity preferable to math, except when the teacher yells at him or tears up his drawings. Does the mother have a problem? No, the behavior occurs in the teacher's environment. The parent may be made to feel guilty and, therefore, decide to "own" the problem by saying she will talk to the boy; but in this case the teacher owns the problem, and feels frustrated at not being able to solve it.

Mother: "Billy never brings any papers home."

This is the mother's problem. *She* wants Billy to bring the papers home. The teacher may agree that this should happen and may be willing to help Billy's mother solve the problem, but it remains Billy's mother's problem.

Cathy: "You never let me be first to get a drink."

Cathy has expressed *her* problem of not being first to get a drink. The teacher may be able to help Cathy resolve the problem, but Cathy still owns it.

Phil: "The kids on the playground knocked me down."

The teacher may be inclined to accept ownership of this problem and intervene, but it is still Phil's problem. The above solution does not help Phil analyze (1) what he does before he is knocked down—the stimulus condition, or (2) what he does after he has been knocked down—the consequence condition.

The most successful resolution of problems requires participants to come to grips with who owns the problem. Outside agents—the federal government, the courts, the school administration, or the power of parents—may *resolve* the problem, but the individual who owns the problem will not likely learn to be a successful problem solver until he/she acknowledges ownership.

Teachers must recognize which problems are theirs, which ones are the child's, and which ones are the parents'. Through active listening, teachers can often determine who has the problem. Confronting a parent or child by saying, "That's your problem" is seldom useful, but by not assuming ownership of the problem, teachers often can help a parent or a child realize that it is his/her problem to solve.

HOW DOES ONE IDENTIFY THE PROBLEM?

Many of the terms used in special education are so global that they do not lend themselves to modification procedures. To say that a child is gifted, retarded, disturbed, or hyperactive is not particularly descriptive of the child's behaviors. When a parent or a teacher uses a term such as "irresponsible" in describing a child, he/she usually has in mind one or two specific behaviors that prompted use of the label. Perhaps the child who is labeled irresponsible has left her bicycle at school, did not take a pencil to class, or does not feed his dog. Some observable behaviors do not occur often enough to satisfy the observer or, in the case of children who are labeled "hyperactive," they occur too often.

The step that is indicated, then, is to help the owner of the problem reduce the problem to behaviors that can be observed and measured. This usually can be done by listening to the person who has the problem and listing the behaviors he/she uses to describe the problem. To return to the example of Miss Rogers' concern with Johnny's spelling perform-ance, she might feel that Johnny does not work long enough on study-ing his spelling words, he does not write them legibly, or that he gets only 50% of his words correct on a spelling test. Each of these behaviors is observable and measurable. She can keep records on how long Johnny attends to his spelling words when the children are assigned study time, or on the number of words he writes legibly, or on the percentage of the words he spells correctly on the spelling test. Any of these measures will tell Miss Rogers if she is making progress in solving her problem of "getting Johnny to work on his spelling." If the problem is reduced to measurable terms, the observer should be able to collect data in one of the following ways.

1. *Number of Occurrences.* How many pages did the child read? How many problems were worked correctly? How many times did Tommy hit his sister? These are all examples that allow data to be collected in terms of number of occurrences.
2. *Duration.* How long did Johnny work on the assignment? How long did it take him to arrive at the breakfast table after he was called in the morning?
3. *Percent.* What percent of the problems were correct? What percentage of times Cathy was asked a question in arithmetic did she answer correctly?
4. *Rate.* How many times was Billy out of his seat without permission in an hour? How many words did he read per minute?

A good test of whether the problem has been reduced to a *solvable* problem is whether it can be measured in one of the four ways mentioned. If the problem cannot be put into measurable terms, one will have difficulty determining when and if the problem has been solved.

In helping a parent define a problem, the teacher usually goes through a number of steps. These are not necessarily followed sequentially, but the teacher may use them as guides.

1. Reduce a global problem into measurable problems.
2. Check your listening by restating the measurable problem to make sure it is what the parent meant to say.
3. List the "new problems" on a sheet of paper.
4. Ask the parent to establish a priority list of the problems he/she would like to work on.
5. With the parent, determine how that particular behavior might be measured.

Perhaps the following example will help clarify the procedure.

Mother:	Billy makes me so mad. He never remembers to bring things home. He keeps me in the dark.
Teacher:	He never brings things home?
Mother:	I haven't seen any of his school papers or PTA notices. If you hadn't called me, I wouldn't have known about this meeting.
Teacher:	Anything else that he doesn't bring home?
Mother:	He left his bike someplace yesterday, and I don't know where his coat is.

Teacher: Let's see. You said he doesn't bring home his papers from school, PTA notices, his bike, or his coat. Is that about it?

Mother: That's mainly it.

Teacher: Let me write them down.
a. school papers
b. notices from school
c. bike
d. coat
Now which of those things would you like to work on first?

Mother: The school papers. Really, the bike and the coat are not big problems because he usually brings them home. He just forgets them once in a while. I guess all together they just seemed like an overwhelming problem.

Teacher: But they are not so big when we break them down?

Mother: No, but I would like to do something about the school papers so I could see what he's doing at school.

Teacher: I usually send papers home on Monday, Wednesday, and Friday. For the next 2 weeks why don't you keep track on your calendar at home on those days? After you have an accurate record of what he's doing, we'll see if we can't set up a program to help get those papers home.

In this instance, the mother was able, with the teacher's help, to break the problem down to a managable size. The teacher checked her perceptions with the mother and found them to be accurate. They listed the problems and established a priority. The teacher then set up a procedure for the mother to start recording the behavior in a simple way.

Being a good listener is often not enough. Parents need help in specifying their problems and establishing strategies to deal with those problems (Bersoff & Grieger, 1971; Krumboltz & Thoresen, 1969). Some problems may not be appropriate for the teacher to deal with in that they are not school-related or they are so deep-seated that other professionals would be better qualified to help solve them. As the problems begin to unfold, it may become obvious to the teacher that the parent should be referred to outside agencies. Wise teachers work on problems they can help identify and help solve, and are willing to turn over to others the problems that are not in their own area of expertise.

DETERRENTS TO PROBLEM IDENTIFICATION _____

A number of deterrents to problem identification are mentioned here. Some have already been identified and should be reiterated. Others may be less easily recognizable.

1. Unwillingness to accept or allow ownership of a problem is a major deterrent to problem identification. Rather than acknowledging that they have a problem, some parents say, "I have a friend whose son still wets the bed." The teacher may decide not to push the parent for ownership at this time but, rather, proceed through the steps of problem identification, which makes the process a bit more difficult. Equally difficult is the situation in which the teacher decides to take over a problem that should be the parents' to solve. When the parent might need to learn how to identify a problem and how to apply reinforcement techniques to solve the problem, sometimes the teacher steps in and ensures that the problem is resolved. In the earlier case of Billy, the teacher might have said, "I'll just not send home any papers and you won't have to worry about it. I'll keep them until the next conference or send them in the mail." This is not conducive to real problem solving.

2. Another deterrent to an accurate definition of the problem is the use of labels to describe the child. Using labels for children in special education has become so common that labeling has lost its original purpose—as being *descriptive* of behavior—and instead is viewed as being a *cause* of behavior. In so doing, many problems that could be reduced to measurable terms are ignored because they are considered to be part of the larger syndrome and are "caused" by the label. For instance, a teacher may say, "Most brain damaged children are hyperactive." Following this line of thought, the teacher feels no need to try to break the word "hyperactive" into measurable entities. Categorical labeling, then, can be a deterrent to problem identification.

3. Heredity is used at times as an excuse not to identify a behavior for problem solving. Problems are sometimes thought to exist as inherited traits. If a child fights on the playground, the teacher or the parent may say, "It's in his blood." They might

say the same of poor math performance or discourteous behavior. If the behavior is explained away by heredity, chances are great that no further attempt will be made to define the problem in behavioral terms. The problem has been "solved" by relegating it to an accident of birth.

4. Sometimes parents or teachers simply do not see a problem, or if they do, they refuse to admit it. In the course of a conference, a parent may say that he/she has to continually keep the child away from matches. In the next sentence the parent may say that this is not really a problem because all children like to play with fire. In this case, the teacher does not own the problem since it does not occur in his/her environment. The child enjoys lighting fires, and the parent refuses to admit that a problem exists.

Problem identification is not always an easy task. It has many deterrents. Parents of exceptional children have many problems to resolve, of which perhaps the greatest is having a handicapped child. Teachers need a great deal of patience to help parents solve some of their day-to-day problems.

SUMMARY

Parents and teachers can work together toward the solution of many problems encountered daily. The first consideration in problem solving is to establish ownership of the problem. At first, this may seem to be a clear-cut step, but parents and teachers tend to want to place the problem in the other's domain.

Second, problem solving is enhanced by being able to reduce global problems into entities that are measurable and observable. Defining behaviors in measurable terms helps place the problem in perspective, takes away some of the subjectivity surrounding the problem, and enables one to more readily determine when the problem has been solved. Teachers who serve as the catalyst in the problem solving conference (1) reduce the problems to measurable terms, (2) restate the problems to verify their perceptions, (3) list the problems, (4) ask that the problems be prioritized, and (5) set up a procedure for measuring the behavior.

Problem identification has a number of deterrents. Unwillingness to accept or allow ownership of the problem makes problem solving difficult. The use of labels as excuses for behavior or the explanation that the behavior is hereditary often prevents the teacher and the parent from coming to grips with problem solving techniques.

Problem identification is not easy, but unless this step is accomplished, proceeding to a solution is difficult, if not impossible. A number of interviews may be required to get to a point where plans for change can be made.

REFERENCES

Bersoff, D.N., & Grieger, R.M. (1971). An interview model for the psychosituational assessment of children's behavior. *American Journal of Orthopsychiatry, 41*, 483-493.
Gordon, T. (1970). *Parent effectiveness training.* New York: Peter H. Wyden.
Krumboltz, J.D., & Thoresen, C.E. (1969). *Behavioral counseling: Cases and techniques.* New York: Holt, Rinehart & Winston.

ACTIVITIES

1. Listen to statements made in the teachers' lounge and see if you can determine "who has the problem."

2. Divide into pairs for role playing. One person is to be the parent and one is the teacher. Break the following down into suitable targets:

    a. The irresponsible child
    b. The hyperactive boy
    c. The lazy girl
    d. The mean boy
    e. The immature child
    f. The anxious child
    g. The nervous child
    h. The shy girl
    i. The retarded girl
    j. The stupid kid.

10

Reinforcers and Reinforcement

Changing child behavior in an environment invariably demands careful analysis of the behavior and the conditions that maintain the behavior. In addition, once a strategy is decided upon, a great deal of effort is demanded of the change agents—in this case, the parents—to maintain the consistency necessary to carry out the plan.

Although teaching parents the ABCs (antecedents, behavior, and consequences) of behavior modification is possible (Haring & Phillips, 1972) in groups or individually, selecting appropriate consequences or reinforcers for the individual child requires knowledge of what "turns the child on." Another concern is how the reinforcers should be applied to be most effective.

WHAT IS A REINFORCER? _____

The words *reinforcer, reward,* and *consequence* have been used interchangeably in behavior modification literature. For something to

132

be reinforcing, it has to follow a specific behavior and to actually have some effect on that behavior—either to accelerate the behavior or to maintain it. Parents sometimes say, "Rewards don't work with my child." By definition, that which they are calling a reward is not a reward. They may be dispensing candy, allowing for additional TV watching, or giving a lot of kisses and hugs for a certain behavior, but if the behavior does not change, those things that the parents are calling rewards are not viewed as rewards, consequences, or reinforcers by the child. In effect, the parent is saying, "I'm doing something that *I* think is rewarding," while the child does not see it as such.

The following points attempt to define and explain reinforcement so that it can be applied with more success.

1. A reinforcer is something that is needed or valued by the recipient and not necessarily something that is valued by the giver. Parents may decide that Billy has done his homework so faithfully that they will let him stay up an extra 15 minutes. Staying up an extra 15 minutes is often rewarding to young children who have a fixed bedtime schedule. In Billy's case, however, he may *need* his sleep; he may not really appreciate the gift of the extra 15 minutes that his parents think is so rewarding. Although he stays up to receive his "reward," the next night he does not do his homework and the parents feel that nothing works. For Billy, being able to sleep an extra 15 minutes in the morning or to sleep in on Saturday mornings may be more rewarding.

   Parents are often surprised at Christmas or on birthdays when a child opens several "neat" presents and puts them aside to play with some inexpensive toy. And they sometimes become disconcerted, after traveling hundreds of miles on a vacation trip to see some historical monument, to realize that the children are more enthusiastic about the swimming pool at the motel. A child may remember for years the time he got to sleep in a dresser drawer and barely remember the magnificence of Niagara Falls, which was viewed during the same trip.

   Rewards are relative to the needs and values of the recipient. A safety pin to a boy who has just broken his zipper is much more rewarding at that moment than a $10 gift certificate to the local department store. Whose values or needs are being met or are being considered when a "reward" is given? Adults, parents, and teachers sometimes think in terms of what they consider reinforcing rather than what the child considers a treat. Before stating that a child is not affected by rewards, one should analyze what is rewarding to the child.

2. A reward must be timely. "Study hard in kindergarten and you can go to college" or, "If you don't smoke until you are 21, I'll buy you a gold watch" are examples of rewards that do not have a reinforcing quality because of the long delay between the behavior desired and the consequence that is supposed to motivate it. The promise of rewards in heaven for good behavior on earth obviously has not had a tremendous effect on humankind.

   Parents sometimes select rewards that are truly reinforcers to children in that the child needs or values them, but by placing them so far in the future, they lose their motivating quality. Therefore, if a parent says that rewards don't work because "Even the promise of a motorcycle did not result in better grades" reflects a lack of knowledge about timing and the need for understanding behavioral principles as they relate to a single child.

   If they are associated closely in time to the behavior, smaller rewards may be much more reinforcing than larger rewards that are poorly timed. A soft drink immediately after the lawn is raked could have a much greater effect on raking behavior than the promise of a case of soft drinks if the lawn is maintained all fall.

3. The applied consequence must be directly associated with the behavior to be changed. Some children have difficulty in seeing a relationship between the behavior and its consequences. This may result when the consequences for a particular behavior are sometimes positive and sometimes negative or when the rewards are dispensed regardless of whether the desired behavior occurs.

   As a small child ventures into the neighborhood, he/she often gets involved in minor scraps with other neighborhood children. The incidents may relate to possession of toys, dissention about games to play, and so forth. In any event, a fight or quarrel ensues and the child goes home. On one occasion the father may demonstrate pride: "That's my son—a chip off the old block." The child may receive a lot of "social rewards" for fighting with the neighbor boy. In a sense he is made to feel good, and fighting is reinforced. Under these conditions, one could expect the fights to continue. The next day, however, the other child's father may call and complain about the fighting. This time the child is punished and sent to his room for fighting. The inconsistency of one day being rewarded and the next day being punished is confusing for the child and does not allow him/her to see the relationship between behavior and its consequences.

In the second case—rewards being dispensed regardless of whether the behavior occurs—a child may be told that she can watch a favorite TV program if she gets her homework done. If time for the program arrives and the child is not finished with her homework but the parent decides to let her watch the program anyway, the child sees no relationship between studying and TV watching. The parents then may say that watching a favorite program does not seem to have any effect on doing homework, and in this case they will be right—because no relationship has been established. Unkept promises such as those mentioned above appear to have a negative effect on children. Children are more affected by what we do than by what we say. If the parent did not enforce the homework/TV contract, it would have been better left unstated. To say that the child will not work for the reward of watching TV is unfair if the child never has had a chance to do so.

Reinforcers, rewards, or consequences are such only if they change behavior. Events or things that are labeled rewards by the giver may have no reinforcing value to the child. For a reward to effect change, it must have value to or be needed by the recipient, it must be timely, and it must have an association with the desired behavior.

SELECTION OF REINFORCERS _____

Selecting things, events, or activities that have reinforcing qualities for another person sometimes presents quite a challenge. Not all children like to be read to, stay up late, ride horses, bake cookies, or whatever. A child from a rural area may have different needs than a child from an inner city area. Young children want rewards different from older children.

Sometimes rewards are the lesser of two evils. A child might find washing the car more rewarding than washing the dishes. Likewise, getting out of some activity might be more rewarding than getting to do something special. For instance, Bill might be told that if he eats the food on his plate, he won't have to wash the dishes that day (which is a regularly assigned task). Just as children differ in so many of their behaviors, so do their rewards and reinforcers vary. Therefore, one must study the child and his/her individual needs.

1. *Observe the child.* Although suggesting to parents that they go home and watch their child to see what he/she likes to do sounds trite, this is probably one of the best ways to determine a reward system. Watching the foods children select, the games or toys they play with longest, where they ask to go, TV programs they like to watch, the types of books they pick to read, furniture they prefer to sit in, and the children they like to play with provide indications of what is rewarding to specific children.

   Parents might check out potential reinforcers by suggesting a trip to the store, walking through a toy department, going for a ride, then observing the child's reaction to the various things he/she encounters. In this way one can build up a reservoir of rewards to be used in various circumstances. By observing the child in a number of different situations, the parents can learn to understand their child better. Sometimes they come back to the teacher with new outlooks about themselves and their children. Occasionally, as they study their child, they find that the behavior under question is really not as important as they had originally thought.

2. *Ask the child.* Just as asking the child what behavior he/she would like to change may be a good idea, asking the child what reward he/she would like for changing this behavior may be effective. Then the parents and the child can come to an agreement about what reinforcers to use for improved school behavior.

   The obvious advantage to this procedure is that it instills some commitment to change, in that the child puts his her own price on the effort. The obvious disadvantage is that our rewards often are so much a part of our everyday living that we do not think of them. Using the Reinforcement Questionnaire (Appendix D) gives children an opportunity to think about a variety of things that turn them on or off. The "asking the child" procedure, as is the observation technique of point 1, is limited by the immediate experiences of the child and parents.

3. *Create reinforcers.* As the story goes, an American firm was producing a product in a developing nation. Employment of local labor was necessary to make the product available. After a while production began to lag, and one day very few workers showed up. The American supervisor asked the local foreman what the problem was. Wages seemed adequate, working con-

ditions were good, most of the people seemed happy, but something was missing.

The local foreman told the supervisor that his people were happy and did not want more money or shorter hours. It was just that most of them had earned all the money they needed to buy supplies, new knives, and their needs were fulfilled. They would be back when they needed money, but in the meantime they were well satisfied. Although this was a happy state for the local workers, it was not doing anything for production. The American supervisor pondered the problem and finally came up with a solution. He had department store catalogs sent to every local household!

Quite often things become *needs* only after they are placed before our eyes or are presented to us. Many of our so-called needs are acquired over time. New foods are found to be pleasurable; activities take on a new meaning when one becomes skilled or when they are associated with friends.

Many times a child needs to be reinforced or rewarded to learn a new skill, but when the new skill is learned it becomes a reward in itself. Consider, for example, a small boy learning to ride a bicycle. His father pushes him and runs along beside him shouting words of encouragement. Each new accomplishment receives a tremendous amount of social reinforcement. After the boy learns to ride without falling off, the riding itself becomes reinforcing and can be used as a reward for other behaviors. The mother may say, "When you finish feeding the dog, you may ride your bike." Many skills that children work hard to achieve—reading, driving, swimming, dancing, piano playing—become reinforcers later on.

Sometimes the way that an activity is presented to a child helps create its reinforcing value. A mother wanted her daughter to learn to play the piano. Because piano practice often becomes a hassle, the mother took a different tack. In the beginning she told her daughter that if she finished her chores, she could practice for 5 minutes. At the end of 5 minutes, the mother stopped the practice. The mother kept track in a little notebook of the number of minutes the girl practiced. Before long the daughter was asking to practice more. The mother slowly allowed the length of time to increase, usually stopping it before the child was satiated and almost always using practice as a privilege for getting other things done. In this way, piano practice was created as a reward or reinforcer, whereas in many homes the child has to be reinforced for practicing. To hear, "When you've finished your half hour of practice, you can go out to play" is much more common.

How something is presented—whether it will be received as a positive or negative event—is important. Note, for instance, in the adult world when one is accorded a great deal of fanfare ("You have been selected to be chairperson of the Fund Raising Committee"—a perfectly laborious task that is often accompanied by more criticism than praise), people accept the job, because it is *presented* as a privilege or "reward."

TYPES OF REINFORCERS

Some authors make distinctions between tangible and social rewards (Clarizio, 1971) or unlearned, social, token, and activity reinforcers (Becker, 1971). Tangible rewards consist of *things* a person receives for accomplishment. They may be learned or unlearned reinforcers, such as money (learned) and food (unlearned). Tangibles are often things the child can keep that serve as reminders of specific achievement for some time to come. Parents and teachers often criticize the use of tangible rewards because of the connotation of paying children to do something that they should want to do or should do anyway. It might be argued, however, that almost all behavior is learned and that few things are done without some type of reward or from a fear of punishment.

Consider for a moment the power of tangible rewards. Certificates, diplomas, and awards are tangible rewards. Many business people, doctors, and lawyers prominently display these symbols of achievement in their offices, along with trophies and plaques they have received. Medals, blood donor pins, past-president pins are worn or at least saved and cherished by many adults. Scrapbooks, photo albums, newspaper clippings all reflect the importance people place on tangible things they have received in the past. Children often have a special drawer where they keep trinkets, toys, ribbons, certificates, old report cards, and other symbols of achievement. Few mothers discard mementos received from their children for being a "Super Mother." Tangible rewards obviously are reinforcing for the majority of individuals in our society, because we keep them.

Social rewards are especially potent because they are "carried around" by the parent or teacher, and they can be administered immediately. They can easily be varied in strength and can be changed on the spot. These rewards include verbal words of praise, closeness of person, touches, pats, hugs, kisses, playing games together, taking rides together, and many other things that one person does for or to another. Some people seem to be natural social reinforcers. They are warm, sensitive individuals who respond readily to the accomplishments of others. On the other hand, some parents and teachers need to learn how to play with children and how to openly display affection.

The power of social recognition is well attested to. Teachers often comment about how some children will do anything for attention. The musical show *Applause* points out the importance of applause. Social approval of the home-town crowd is considered crucial in competitive athletic events.

The necessity of making a distinction between types of reinforcers is probably more important to the researcher than it is to the practitioner. Parents are usually more interested in ideas that work than they are in the relative merits of social versus tangible reward systems. Figures 15 and 16 give lists of rewards that parents have found to be effective. They are grouped for younger and older children, but a parent may want to check both lists because of the individual differences of children. Many of the items on the lists are free or inexpensive. Rewards do, however, take time. And *how one presents* the potential reinforcer is crucial.

SUMMARY

New patterns of behavior are learned through a process of reinforcement. A reinforcer, reward, or consequence is something that follows a behavior in such a way that the recipient sees a relationship between the behavior and its consequences; it is well-timed; and it is valued or needed by the recipient. The applied consequence can be considered a reinforcer only if it changes the behavior in some way.

Figuring out how to select reinforcers that the child will find rewarding can be done in a number of ways. One way is to observe the child in a loosely controlled environment to see what he/she prefers to do or to play with when given a free choice. Another way is to ask the child what he/she would like to have or to do. Sometimes reinforcers have to be created by providing children with new experiences or things that they have not experienced before.

Some educators classify reinforcers or rewards as learned and unlearned, or as tangible and social, or as social, token, and activity rewards. These classification systems are probably of less importance to practitioners (parents and teachers) than they are to researchers. One of

REWARDS FOR YOUNGER CHILDREN

★ Being read to
★ Riding on a horse with Dad or Mom
★ Getting a bubble pipe
★ Helping make cookies
★ Playing tic-tac-toe with Mom or Dad
★ Listening to a favorite record
★ Watching a favorite TV show
★ Staying up an extra 15 minutes
★ Going for ice cream in pajamas
★ Putting special papers on the wall or refrigerator
★ Getting a subscription to a magazine
★ Getting a dog, a cat, a fish, a gerbil
★ Choosing a new shirt or blouse
★ Visiting a TV station or fire station
★ Selecting something special at the grocery store
★ Calling Grandma long distance
★ Making popcorn
★ Getting to help wash dishes (very young!)
★ Getting out of washing dishes (older)
★ Getting stars, gummed stickers, etc.
★ Using Mom's makeup
★ Getting homemade certificates or awards for "Super Helper"
★ Getting pipe cleaners, paper clips to make things
★ Having a big box to play in
★ Undertaking various responsibilities: feeding pet, taking out trash, turning out lights, safety inspection
★ Having overnight guests
★ Going to a movie
★ Using "grown-up" tools
★ Enjoying a specified (in writing) amount of Dad's or Mom's time
★ Playing games
★ Getting pats, hugs, kisses
★ Going to a friend's house
★ Buying comic books
★ Using a kitchen timer or a stopwatch
★ Having a chart with checkmarks for completing tasks
★ Getting balloons
★ Doing things first—like reading the comics in the paper
★ Setting the table
★ Having free time
★ Getting a new bedspread or Snoopy blanket
★ Having a pint of ice cream of one's very own
★ Getting a library card

FIGURE 15
Reinforcement Ideas for Younger Children

REWARDS FOR OLDER CHILDREN

★ Attending a rock concert
★ Having a party
★ Having telephone privileges
★ Staying up late on Friday or Saturday
★ Using the car
★ Having own set of car keys or house keys
★ Getting books
★ Taking driver's training
★ Buying new clothes
★ Having extra money
★ Getting black light for room
★ Buying posters
★ Rearranging furniture in room
★ Watching Late Late Show
★ Taking a friend out to dinner
★ Going to a movie, skating, or other event
★ Taking special lessons: Dancing, skiing, scuba diving
★ Going on a picnic
★ Playing chess, cribbage, bridge, computer games
★ Having friends overnight
★ Getting a pet
★ Building something with a parent
★ Having a friend stay over for the weekend
★ Keeping a graph or chart of one's progress
★ Getting a new record album or tape
★ Getting out of specified chores
★ Having dates
★ Physical contact, touches, etc. (this is often missing with older children)
★ Taking trips to special places
★ Getting flowers
★ Getting a magazine subscription
★ Getting materials for rebuilding a car, radio, TV, etc.
★ Going to camp
★ Enjoying special snacks
★ Reading to younger children
★ Having "goof off" time with *no* responsibilities
★ Getting one's picture taken
★ Going to the library
★ Getting breakfast in bed

FIGURE 16
Reinforcement Ideas for Older Children

the major advantages of encouraging parents to establish the value of social reinforcers (kisses, hugs, words of praise) with the child, however, is that parents have these with them at all times. Thus, if children have learned to value the social rewards of significant adults in their lives, these reinforcers can be applied immediately and they can be directly related to the child's behavior.

REFERENCES

Becker, W.C. (1971). *Parents are teachers*. Champaign, IL: Research Press.
Clarizio, H. (1971). *Toward positive classroom discipline*. New York: John Wiley & Sons.
Haring, N., & Phillips, E.L. (1972). *Analysis and modification of classroom behavior*. Englewood Cliffs, NJ: Prentice-Hall.

ACTIVITIES

1. Observe a child with whom you have contact, and make a list of the things that he/she seems to prefer to do. Ask the child to list the things that he/she would like to have or do, and compare them with your observations. You may want to use the Reinforcement Questionnaire (Appendix D) for this activity.

2. If you are a teacher, ask the children in your class to prepare a list of things they like to do or have at school or at home. From these lists make a single list of your own to have available to share with parents as ideas for reinforcers.

3. Develop certificates or awards that parents might use with their children at home for specific behaviors—helping clean the kitchen, washing dishes for a week, making the bed, etc.

11

The Reinforcement Menu

Parents usually understand the use of positive reinforcers to influence or change behavior. Having lived with the child for a number of years, they have observed how the child cleans up his/her room in order to go someplace in the truck or helps with the dishes in order to go to a movie. They've watched their child save pennies to buy a certain toy. In a conference between teacher and parents, the teacher usually needs only to mention some of these probable occurrences for the parents to understand the behavior principles involved. Dealing with examples and staying away from technical jargon are usually the most productive ways of helping parents.

Parents tend to carry out many mini-mods (miniature modifications) but seldom plan systematically to carry on long-term behavior change projects. Getting the lawn raked today or the car washed tomorrow or the bedroom cleaned on Saturday are on-the-spot behaviors that are dealt with at the time. "You may use the car tonight if you wash it this afternoon" is a mini-mod. Problems occur when an undesirable behavior, such as tantrum behavior, bedwetting, or not getting up in the morning when called, persists over time. Although the same principles that were used to get the lawn raked are applicable to getting the child up in the morning, they must be applied consistently and over time to effect behavior change. This is when parents need help in establishing a strategy.

In the last chapter the selection and application of reinforcers was discussed. The reinforcers identified can be used for both short-term projects and in the more difficult long-term problem solving procedures. One strategy for dealing with persistent behaviors is to establish a reinforcement menu for the child (Clarizio, 1971; Edlund, 1969; Homme, 1969). A reinforcement menu is simply a number of reinforcers from which the child can choose when he/she has earned the required number of points. Each reinforcer has previously been assigned a point value. The following procedure demonstrates how to set up and carry out a program for behavior change using the reinforcement menu strategy.

DEFINING THE BEHAVIOR

During the parent-teacher conference, Mrs. Smith complained that her son, Phil, was so lazy that it was getting on her nerves. She was always yelling at him, and she had to tell him four or five times to do required chores. The teacher, Mrs. Rogers, realized that "lazy" meant many different things to different people and that getting a grasp on it would be difficult unless it was defined in more behavioral terms. She asked Mrs. Smith what she meant by saying that Phil was lazy.

"He won't get up when I call him in the morning, and I have to tell him over and over again to take out the trash."

"Anything else?"

"He wanted a dog so bad, and he got it, but now he forgets to feed the dog and I have to remind him or do it myself."

"Yes..."

"He seldom makes his bed without being told. I suppose he's just going through a stage, but I'm tired of it."

"Even if it's a stage he's going through, I imagine you'd like to do something about it."

"You bet! But what I'm doing now sure isn't working."

"Let's see if I can help. This is a method that one of the mothers tried last year, and she said it worked for her."

Mrs. Rogers made a list of the behaviors that Mrs. Smith had called "lazy."

1. Get up in the morning when called.
2. Take out the trash.
3. Feed the dog.
4. Make his bed.

Mrs. Rogers then asked, "Are these the main things that are getting on your nerves?"

"Well, there are a few others, but those are the most bothersome to me and his dad."

"Do you want each of them to take place every day?"

"No, I don't care if he sleeps in on Saturday and Sunday, and the trash has to be taken out only on Tuesday and Friday, but I wish he's do the others every day."

Mrs. Rogers said, "Let's make a chart for him that will help to remind him."

She then sketched out a work chart (see Figure 17).

"Mrs. Smith, Phil probably needs a little help to remind him of what he should do and when he should do it. If we make a little chart like this and put it on the door of his room, he'll be able to see what he's supposed to do. Then you can check it off with the assigned number of points when he's done. You can make any task worth as many points as you want to, depending on how important the task is. For instance, if you really want him to make his bed, you might make that worth more points."

"What if he doesn't make his bed until just before he gets back into it that night?"

"You'll have to decide with him what you consider to be a deadline time for the points to be earned and then stick to it."

"I see. Is that all there is to it?"

"No, I think we need to make the points worth something, don't you?"

PREPARING A POINT RECORD SHEET _____

The next step is to develop some type of "accounting system." Because Mrs. Smith and Mrs. Rogers had developed a plan for Phil to earn points and they were going to develop a plan for spending the points, they both felt that some type of procedure should be developed so that Phil could keep track of the points he had available.

Week ———

Supervisor ———

	Monday	Tuesday	Wednesday	Thursday	Friday	Saturday	Sunday
1. Gets up when called							
2. Takes out trash							
3. Feeds dog							
4. Makes bed							
5.							
6.							
7.							
TOTAL POINTS							

1. Gets up when called once = 10 pts.
   Gets up when called twice = 5 pts.
   Doesn't respond = 0 pts.
2. Takes out trash = 10 pts.
3. Feeds dog = 10 pts.
4. Makes bed = 10 pts.

Total Possible ———

Total Earned ———

FIGURE 17
Phil's Work Record

The parent can use any of a number of systems, depending on the age of the child and how much work one wants done. One teacher, for instance, made individual checkbooks for her students. They deposited the points they earned into their checking account. If a student wanted a particular item or event, he/she wrote a check for the required number of points and subtracted that from the balance. In this way, the students practiced handling a checking account, and they used the arithmetic skills of adding and subtracting.

Phil's mother and Mrs. Rogers decided on a rather simple record sheet (Figure 18) to help Phil keep track of his points. It had five columns: one for the date, one for the points earned on that date, one for the points spent (if any), one for the points he had for a balance, and one to note what he spent the points for. This notation would give Mrs. Smith an indication of what seemed to be strong reinforcers for Phil. By checking the dates on which he spent points, she could see if he was learning to save or whether he needed more immediate gratification.

PREPARING A REINFORCEMENT MENU _____

The next step is to prepare a reinforcement menu. One of the benefits of preparing a list from which Phil could select items was that Mrs.

Date	Points Earned	Points Spent	Points on Hand	Points Spent For

FIGURE 18
Point Record

Smith did not have to try to determine the single most reinforcing event for him. A number of items could be placed on the menu, each with its own price tag, and Phil could make up his own mind about how he wanted to use his points. In addition, the list could be changed periodically just as a menu is changed at a restaurant. The "prices" can also be altered if deemed necessary.

Mrs. Smith and Mrs. Rogers went through the process described in the previous chapter for selecting reinforcers. They relied on their observations of what Phil seemed to like to do or have, then asked Phil for suggestions as to what he would like to work for, using some of the questions found on the Reinforcement Questionnaire (Appendix D). In addition, they looked through the list of possible reinforcers found in Figure 15 of the previous chapter. They came up with the following list of nine items:

1. Watch TV for 1 hour (maximum 3 hours of TV on weekday)	5 points
2. Go bowling on Saturday	160 points
3. An evening snack	5 points
4. Have a friend stay overnight	180 points
5. A baseball glove	380 points
6. Go to Dad's office	70 points
7. Stay up an extra 15 minutes	Bonus for a perfect Tuesday or Friday
8. Play 10 games of tic-tac-toe with Mom	25 points
9. Not have to do the dishes on Friday (assigned night)	40 points

The various items and their respective point values were derived for a number of reasons. Phil liked to watch TV and have an evening snack almost every day. The low point totals would not cause him to use all of his points on these items but would almost guarantee that he would change at least one of the behaviors that Mrs. Smith would like him to change. Tuesdays and Fridays were the biggest days in that Phil had to take out the trash in addition to getting up in the morning when called, feeding the dog, and making his bed on these days, so a bonus of staying up 15 extra minutes was thrown in as an added incentive. Going bowling or having a friend overnight required a pretty good week. He could not get enough points in a week to do both, but he could do one if he wanted to save his points. The baseball glove was something the family would probably get him eventually, but Phil could earn it in 2 or 3 pretty good weeks by managing his points. If he showed no indication of working for it after a few weeks, it could be replaced by some other big item. Phil had the assigned job of helping with dishes on Friday night, which had often ended up in an argument. By placing a point value on getting out of doing the dishes, the arguing behavior possibly could be reduced. He could buy his way out of the task by spending 40 points, or he could do the dishes. The visit to Dad's office was included just to see if it was a reinforcer for Phil.

The list was posted for Phil to see. If Phil had been younger, Mrs. Smith might have used pictures of reinforcers instead of the list of words. The next step was to go over the procedures carefully with Phil so that he understood the whole process. It was presented not as a punishment for not doing these things earlier, but as an aid to help Phil remember. The reinforcement menu is like a department store catalog. It tells one what is available and the price it costs.

THINGS TO REMEMBER ─────────────

1. Make sure the process is clear to the child. In the above example, Phil should know what constitutes a "made bed" and when the deadline is. He should know how and when he can spend his points.
2. Don't shift point values. If Phil is working hard to save the 380 points for the baseball glove and the parents discover they have underpriced the item, it is not fair to up the price just before he gets there.
3. Don't offer a reinforcer that you are not willing to give. Parents and teachers sometimes place on a menu an item that looks especially attractive but that they cannot or will not deliver on demand. For instance, a trip to the zoo may be worth 300 points and is promised for the first Saturday after the child has earned the points. The Saturday in question arrives, but Dad has a golf game scheduled and Mom has bridge. After working 3 weeks for the trip to the zoo, the child should not be denied, except under unquestionable circumstances. Otherwise the reinforcer should not be listed. Don't break a contract with a defenseless child.
4. Be consistent in administering the program. If the child has not earned the necessary points for TV watching, don't give in, even "just this once." On the other hand, if Suzy has the points for having a friend overnight, don't deny her because she spilled her soup. Being consistent is difficult, but the lack of consistency often caused the problem in the first place.

5. Continually evaluate the program. By analyzing the Work Record (Figure 17), the parent can see what is working and what is not working. For instance, Phil might be earning enough points to satisfy his immediate needs by doing some of the tasks on the chart and not doing others. Maybe he still is not feeding the dog on a regular basis, but Mrs. Smith would like to see this happen. She can do a number of different things. She might increase the amount of points that Phil can earn for this activity and thereby make it worth more. She might add another reinforcer that is especially desirable and, therefore, Phil has to earn more points to get it. She might eliminate one of the tasks on the chart that seems to have become a habit and, thus, make it necessary for Phil to feed the dog to get enough points to live in the style to which he has become accustomed.

Mrs. Smith should evaluate the effectiveness of the reinforcers on the menu. If some of them are not being used, she may either want to exchange them for new ones or decrease their point value.

6. Consult with the child. Involving the child in much of the decision making has several direct benefits. It can help him/her understand the process. The child's choice of reinforcers can help parents see what is important to him/her. As points are renegotiated for reinforcers and if children feel they have some input to the program, they will obviously have more commitment to its success. By taking them through the process, they will learn new ways to order their own lives.

> A little girl who was being reinforced with gold stars for sleeping *between* the sheets in her bed told her mother that she wanted to teach her dog to eat his food. Her mother thought that was a good idea and asked her how she was going to do it. "By giving Blackie a gold star every time he cleans up his dish," the girl replied. She understood the process. She just had the wrong reinforcer.

Children usually understand the procedures even if the techniques are not explained, but they will do better if they are taken along on the whole process.

7. Make the program positive. Programs have a better chance of succeeding if they are based on a reward system rather than a punishment system. In Phil's case, if Mrs. Smith had chosen to look at the unmade bed as a target and had set up a system wherein a specified number of unmade beds led to his staying in his

room or no TV, the stage would have been set for a power struggle and the whole project would have been viewed negatively. The reinforcement menu system should be viewed as a tool to reduce conflict between the parent and child through positive means rather than increasing hostility through punishment procedures.

Setting up a program to change home behavior using a reinforcement menu can be exciting. Most parents are willing to try it if the teacher will take the time to help them set it up. A Work Record Form and a Point Record Sheet are given in Appendix E. Teachers might want to use these in helping parents set up a program using the reinforcement menu strategy.

CASE STUDY _____

The following case study illustrates use of the reinforcement menu technique with a child who had temper tantrums. A graduate student worked with the mother to set up and carry out the program. Some of the items and names have been changed slightly in the interests of the child.

> Tad's mother came to the clinic because of her son's "uncontrollable temper tantrums." Tad was of school age, and Mrs. Y was concerned because Tad persisted in getting his own way at the most inconvenient times either by throwing a temper tantrum or by threatening to throw one. A graduate student was assigned to the case and worked closely with the mother throughout the project.
> For a week Mrs. Y was asked to keep track of the number of temper tantrums Tad threw each day. The first week Tad averaged 3.42 tantrums a day (see Figure 19). The mother and the graduate student then developed a point system and a menu of reinforcers (Figure 20). The point system was set up around a plan for *losing* 5 points for each temper tantrum and *earning* points for other behaviors.
> The worksheet (Figure 21) and the point system were explained to Tad. The mother was encouraged not to react to the temper tantrum with anything other than the 5-point deduction. During the next 8 days, the average dropped to .5 times a day. At this point, the mother quit the point system for a 9-day period, and the tantrums increased to an average of 1.7 times a day. A reinstatement of the reinforcement system reduced the number of tantrums to only two for the next 7 days.

Concentrating on the positive aspects of the child's behavior and establishing a point system appeared to have positive effects on the

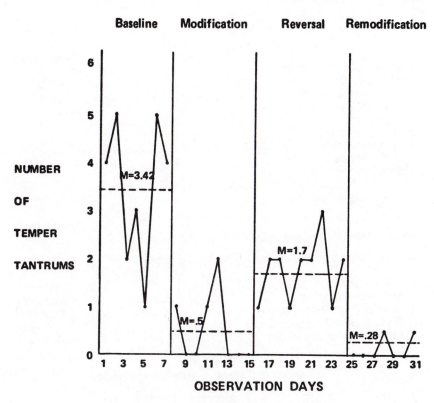

FIGURE 19
Graph of Tad's Temper Tantrums

child's behavior. It was also effective in getting Tad to do some other chores that the mother felt were important. The "uncontrollable temper tantrums" became controllable through a positive systematic approach.

SUMMARY

Parents usually understand the use of positive reinforcement to alter behavior, especially if they are given examples illustrating the principles. Although they have used these techniques to deal with many short-term projects, they have seldom followed a plan to systematically develop habits in their child's behavioral pattern.

One method for systematically changing a child's behavior utilizes the reinforcement menu. First the parent identifies one or a small

To earn points, you may do the following:

Plus Points

1. Keep your room in order
   bed made 5
   dresser arranged neatly 5
   clothes put away 5
   toys put away 5
2. Do home chores
   empty trash 5
   do dishes 5
3. Practice the horn
   each 10 minutes 5
4. Complete school work 5

Minus Points

For each temper tantrum, you lose: 5

You may spend points on the following privileges:

1. Go bowling .... 500 points
2. $1.00 for shopping .... 400 points
3. Stay all night with a friend .... 300 points
4. Dad plays with you .... 200 points
5. Make goodies with mom .... 100 points

FIGURE 20
Point System and Menu of Reinforcers for Tad

POINTS EARNED WEEK OF _____

	Sat.	Sun.	Mon.	Tues.	Wed.	Thur.	Fri.
Bed							
Dresser							
Clothes							
Toys							
Trash							
Dishes							
Horn							
Homework							
Minus points							
Sum							

SUM CARRIED OVER _____
This week's sum _____
CUMULATIVE TOTAL _____

FIGURE 21
Worksheet for Tad

number of behaviors that he/she would like the child to change or do. Each behavior is assigned a point value. Then a system is developed for keeping track of the points the child earns and spends. The third step is to select a number of events that appear to have reinforcing value to the child. Each event is assigned a point value. The points a child earns can be spent to obtain the reinforcers. The list of reinforcers and their values comprise the reinforcement menu.

The process should be clearly understandable to the child. Once the point values have been established, they should not be altered arbitrarily. The reinforcers should be obtainable. The program should be administered consistently, and it should be continually evaluated to make sure it is accomplishing its objectives. Best results will be realized if the child is consulted about the total program and involved in its implementation. Above all, the program should be positive.

REFERENCES

Clarizio, H. (1971). *Toward positive classroom discipline.* New York: John Wiley & Sons.
Edlund, C.V. (1969, summer). Rewards at home to promote desirable school behavior. *Teaching Exceptional Children,* pp. 121-127.
Homme, L.H. (1969). *How to use contingency contracting in the classroom.* Champaign, IL: Research Press.

ACTIVITIES

1. Set up a reinforcement menu for a child or children, including a point system whereby they can obtain the reinforcers.

2. Help a parent set up a reinforcement menu at home to change child behaviors that the parent would like to see modified.

12

Parent Training Groups

Do you want to lose weight, learn to meditate, find romance, learn to square dance, grow better flowers, stop smoking, or stop drinking? Clubs, organizations, and groups exist or are being formed for almost any special interest imaginable. Groups for parents of exceptional children are no exception.

In most large communities parents can find groups that have been organized to provide psychotherapy, teach behavior modification principles, help parents learn to listen to their children or to play with them, explore their feelings and attitudes, or deal with being a single parent or children on drugs. The groups serve as a vehicle for problem solving, and almost every philosophical position—psychoanalytical, behavioral, developmental, phenomenological, transactional analysis—is represented.

One might be inclined to be critical of the vast number of different kinds of groups available to parents of exceptional children. Yet, if one holds the position that differential diagnosis should lead to differential treatment, different types of programs for parents are needed to choose from or be referred to. Most of the continuing groups report that their procedures are effective. The fact that they remain in existence indicates that parents find them satisfying.

In addition to the problem areas addressed, groups are often differentiated by the amount of direction the leaders provide, by the underlying assumptions about human behavior, and whether the targets of the group are behavioral or attitudinal (Table 3).

These distinctions may be somewhat artificial when considering what actually takes place in a group. Any given group may proceed from a highly directive type leadership model to a more nondirective posture on the part of the leader. Thorne (1962) implied that the leader always has control of the meeting and that he/she may choose to provide a great deal of direction or relinquish the leadership to group members. He stated that the healthier the personality, the less is the need for strong direction on the leader's part. In addition, some groups that are based on a structural or directive philosophical model, such as a program to train parents in behavior modification principles, may employ nondirective procedures to enable parents to verbalize the targets they want to use for the projects in which they will be engaged during the training program. To make the group effective, a skillful leader often employs techniques developed by various philosophical models.

TABLE 3
Parent Program Structure Continuum

		Structured by Group Participants		Structured by Group Leader
Degree of Leadership	1.	Group leader sets the stage—provides minimal control, accepting type atmosphere.	1.	Strong leadership—often almost an instructional model.
Assumptions	2.1	Given a warm, accepting atmosphere, parents will make appropriate decisions.	2.1	Parents have not been able to make appropriate decisions; therefore, they need specific guidance.
	2.2	Individuals are capable and have free choice.	2.2	Behavior is learned and, therefore, can be taught.
Targets	3.	Feelings and attitudes of participants.	3.	Specific behaviors.

Because of the many types of groups, reviewing all of them here is not possible. Certain programs will be described in some detail because of their potential for use with parents of exceptional children or because of their popularity.

EDUCATIONAL MODULATION CENTER ⎯⎯⎯⎯

The Educational Modulation Center (EMC) in Olathe, Kansas, was established to investigate procedures for providing educationally handicapped children with special educational services in a rural area where few, if any, special classes existed. One small but seemingly significant part of the total program was a strategy to involve parents in the education of their own children.

When regular classroom teachers in the service area felt that a child demonstrated a discrepancy between ability and performance, he she was referred to the EMC for further evaluation. If the teacher's referral was deemed appropriate for the EMC program, both the teacher and the child's parents were required to attend a workshop consisting of four meetings (see Figure 22).

The program was based on behavioral principles of learning theory. The strategy was to teach the participants—parents and teachers—how to modify behavior, preferably academic behavior, using the consequences available to them. Parents and teachers met separately for the first three meetings, and they came together for the final meeting to share the results of their work. The knowledge that they were to show each other the results of their work at the fourth meeting probably increased the number of successful projects.

Following is a brief summary of the content of the four parent meetings:

1. The parent group consisted of about 25-30 parents, whose children had been referred for services, and 6-10 methods and materials consultants (M & Ms). A brief overview of behavior modification was presented, stressing that behavior is learned and that parents are influential teachers. The M & Ms also stressed that most parents following the planned program would be successful, thus setting a high level of expectancy for success.

   The parents were then instructed in the importance of selecting measurable and observable targets. They were shown how to proceed from a global label of "laziness" to a more specific target of "not getting up from bed when called." Forms

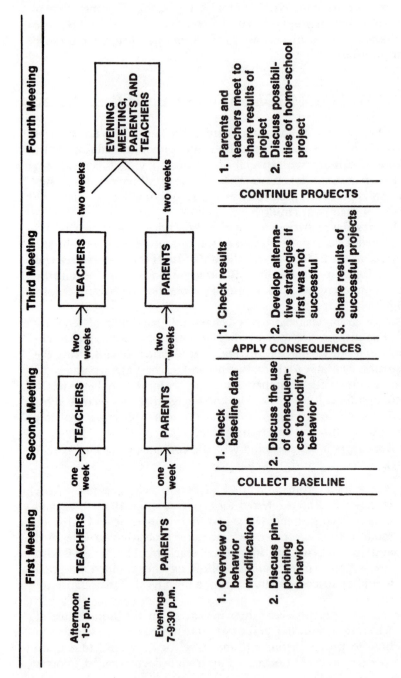

FIGURE 22
EMC Parent-Teacher Workshop Structure

to list behaviors and to place them in priority were given to the parents. Forms were also provided for collecting and recording data. (During the first year of the project, parents usually selected various social behaviors; however, during the second year they were encouraged to select academic targets).

A brief question-and-answer session followed the general presentation. Then the parents met in small groups with the M & Ms to make sure they had selected measurable targets and that they understood how to collect data. They went home with the assignment to collect 1 week of baseline data.

2. The second meeting was held about a week later. If the interval between meetings was more than that, the program sponsors felt, parents might not maintain their interest in data collecting.

The purpose of the second meeting was mainly to teach the parent the ABCs (antecedents, behavior, consequences) of behavior modification. Parents were encouraged to think of the many rewarding conditions and events they already had available in the home—i.e., the child being shown the graphic behavior chart, visual checklists, kitchen timers, extra TV watching, later bedtime, special snacks, allowance.

Usually, several graphs of previous projects that had been successfully carried out by other parents were displayed. A general question-and-answer period followed. Then the parents met in small groups with the M & Ms to graph their baseline data, select a new target if the first was found to be inappropriate, and choose a consequence or develop a plan to alter the antecedent events that may be affecting the child's behavior.

3. The third meeting followed the second by about 2 weeks, to give the parents enough time to notice changes in their child's behavior. The major purposes of the third meeting were to have parents share their successes with each other and to help parents who were having trouble getting an alteration in behavior. The M & Ms reviewed the basic principles, stressing consistency. Much of the period was used by having parents present their projects to the group. This usually resulted in a great deal of peer reinforcement.

Parents who still were not successful or who wanted to work on extra projects met briefly with the M & Ms. They were reinforced for trying and for any successive approximations. The total group was reminded that the next meeting would be with the teachers, to share the results of their work.

4. The fourth meeting, a week or two later, was held jointly between parents and teachers. After a brief general session in

which both groups were praised for their diligence in the program and the success many of them were able to attain, parents and teachers met in small groups with the M & Ms to share the results of their work. These sessions were often quite profitable because teachers and parents were talking a common language. They were able to share with each other the reinforcers that they had found to be effective. Some of the experiences were heartwarming.

> G, a fifth-grade teacher with about 40 years teaching experience, had discovered during the first week of class that David could not read fifth-grade material. She tried third-grade, then first-grade material without much success. She was one of those wonderful teachers who have the self-confidence to truly accept the children at their own level and work with them. When she referred David to the EMC, she was looking forward to the workshop and ways in which she could individualize for David. As her target for David, she selected "being able to identify the letters of the alphabet." By the time of the parent-teacher conference, she had more than accomplished the behavioral objectives, and David was looking forward to coming to school.
>
> The father showed up at the conference in his overalls. He obviously had been working around the farm until just before the meeting. When he sat down with G and the M & Ms, he said to G, "My boy has been looking for you for 5 years."

The results of the EMC project seemed positive (Adamson, 1970). Dr. Richard McDowell, Coordinator for the Program of Behavioral Disorders at the University of New Mexico, did much of the developmental work with the parent program at the EMC. He has since developed a kit for the first three sessions, and the necessary worksheets and forms for the parents to use. Using structured presentations ensures that the important points will be covered and that parents have the necessary information to carry out their homework.

Although parent training programs are regarded as a Level 3 Needs activity in the Mirror Model, these programs can sometimes lead to a Level 4 Strengths activity, by teaching parents to deliver the workshops in which they have participated.

> Shirley was a parent and a grandparent of handicapped children. She enrolled in a parent program on behavior management using the McDowell materials, in a program sponsored by the Parent Involvement Center for the Rehabilitation Center. She was highly successful with her own two charges and seemed to catch on immediately to the principles involved in the program. At the conclusion of the training, she asked if any more sessions were planned.

"Yes, but instead of attending more yourself, how would you like to help us run some other sessions?" we asked.

"I'd love it," she replied.

She started helping us run programs, and the first thing we knew, we were helping her. Next she started helping other teachers in the school system develop and run behavior management programs. We didn't see her for a couple of months. One day she showed up at the Parent Center. She looked terrific.

"Shirley! You look great."

"I've lost 40 pounds. I decided that if I was going to show people how to control behavior, I ought to manage my own. Don't you think you ought to start helping me run these programs again?" she asked, smiling at my obvious roundness.

FILIAL THERAPY

Filial therapy is a parent training program developed by Guerney (1969) to teach parents the principles of play therapy. Although the philosophical base and the underlying assumptions of play therapy are different from those of the behavior modification program, as discussed above, the structure of the program has a number of similarities.

1. In the first stage parents are instructed in the purpose, value, and techniques of play therapy. Demonstration play sessions are conducted, and some role playing techniques are employed. Parents are encouraged to discuss their feelings about their interactions with their children and the techniques they observe.
2. The parents then attempt play therapy with another child or their own child, under supervision. In this way they can discuss what happens during the session and work on their techniques.
3. When the group leader and the parents feel they are ready, the parents begin sessions at home with their own children. They take notes and discuss their feelings about the sessions in their parent group.
4. The final stage is when the group leader and the parents begin to terminate from the program structure. The total program may take from 12 to 16 sessions.

Filial therapy is a program to train small groups of parents to play with their own children. It is hoped that teaching parents to be play therapists with their own children will increase their understanding of children's play and open lines of communication between parents and child.

PARENT COUNSELING GROUPS ⸻

A number of investigations have reported beneficial results from group counseling (Keppers & Caplan, 1962; McCowan, 1968). The emphasis of the program is usually on the affective domain, and non-directive counseling techniques are employed. The content of the meetings is the responsibility of group members, and the group leader tries to reflect the feelings expressed by the participants.

From the findings of McCowan (1968), working with the parents appears to be just as effective as working with the students. Of course, if one has the time, working with both groups is usually the most beneficial. McCowan found that students' grade point averages improved significantly, that attitudes as measured by the California Study Methods Survey improved, and that significant change on some of the scales of the Adjustment Inventory occurred.

PARENT EFFECTIVENESS TRAINING ⸻

The Parent Effectiveness Training (PET) program, along with filial therapy and many of the behavior modification parent programs, attempts to teach parents to become therapists for their own children. As such, it is an educational approach (Gordon, 1970).

The program consists of an 8-week course for parents, in which they are instructed in the techniques of active listening and problem solving. Parents are taught how to analyze their communication transactions with their children.

The groups are composed of 10 to 12 parents and the group leader. They sit in a circle and are encouraged to express their agreement or disagreement with the ideas of the leader or the other members. Ample opportunity for demonstrations and role playing is present. The program is regarded as a "no-lose" method for raising children. Parents are "coached" in allowing their children to express their feelings, and they are taught how to express their own feelings in an open, honest way with their children.

Analyzing *ownership* of a problem (see chapter 9 for a more complete discussion on that topic) is an important component of this program. Parents are taught the importance of allowing children to accept ownership for problems that belong to the child. By being an active listener (see chapter 3), they can help the child arrive at a solution to his/her own problems.

PET provides methods for mutual problem solving and agreement when parents and child come into conflict over an issue. Solutions arrived at jointly have a higher success rate than those arrived at independently by either party. In this way, neither party loses.

THE PARENT "C" GROUP _____

Another type of parent group is the "C" group, discussed by Dinkmeyer and Carlson (1973). They believe that the most successful programs are those that are directed at practical problems. It is called a "C" group because of the focus on the components of collaboration, consultation, clarification, confrontation, concern and caring, confidentiality, and commitment to change.

The group is kept small, usually six to 10 members plus the group leader. The leader sets the stage with a brief discussion of the theoretical position, and then encourages one of the members to present a practical problem. With a small group the leader tries to get all the members involved, and they are encouraged to share ideas toward the solution of each other's problems. During a session each member is supposed to present a problem, develop a hypothesis about the problem, and propose a tentative solution to take home and apply in trying to solve the problem. A public declaration of commitment to change is thought to be important to the effectiveness of this program.

One of the goals of the group leader is to develop new leaders who can conduct groups. Many professionals recognize that they cannot serve the needs of parents individually. Therefore, teaching others their skills is important. This is usually done by taking the participants through a program and demonstrating the techniques to be used.

ADVANTAGES OF PARENT GROUPS _____

The popularity of parent groups has risen in recent years. Working with a group of parents who have something in common—either the age of the child or a particular exceptionality—has obvious advantages.

1. Parents realize that they are not the only ones with a specific problem. Often a parent who has a child who has been classified as mentally retarded feels that he/she is the only one who has to face this problem.
2. Parents can share their strong emotions with others who understand. Feelings of guilt or anger regarding a handicapped child

are often alleviated when they are expressed in a group meeting. The realization that other members of the group have similar feelings seems to have a therapeutic effect.

3. Parents can share solutions. Parents will often listen to solutions to problems from other members of the group more readily than they will from an outside authority. Knowing that other parents have been confronted with a situation similar to their own and have resolved it with a particular action seems to make the proposed solution more palatable.

4. More parents can be reached in a group than individually. Sometimes the group procedure results in a commitment to change in a number of people in an hour session that might take 5 or 6 hours of the leader's time if approached individually. The group procedure, therefore, promotes efficient use of the leader's time.

Throughout the literature on parent groups, size of the groups is an issue. Usually the recommended number of parents is 10 or fewer. The reason is that interaction within the group is desired, and the possibility for interaction decreases rapidly as the number of individuals increases. For instance, if a group has two people, it allows two interactions, but in a group of seven people, 42 interactions are possible if everyone initiates an interaction with everyone else in the group. With 10 people in a group, 90 different interactions are possible if everyone interacts with everyone else.

The group technique is not a solution to all parents' problems. Some parents need one-to-one contact with the teacher or counselor to resolve a particular problem. On the other hand, group work should not be overlooked as a technique for change.

Many teachers do not feel comfortable leading a group of parents. They would prefer that the leader be someone other than themselves because they feel that parents would not be at ease in a session conducted by their child's teacher. This is a legitimate concern. Parent group meetings are presented as an option for consideration, but not as one that all teachers should feel compelled to adopt for parents in their classroom.

PARENT EDUCATION KITS AND MATERIALS

Because of the popularity of parent groups and the obvious need for training, several parent education programs have been put into kit form. This provides the user or leader with the material necessary to set up and implement a parent group. It can save the leader a lot of planning and preparation time. Most of the programs incorporate audiovisual materials that enhance the presentation.

Professionals who do a great deal of group work tend to individualize the programs by using only parts of "canned" programs or adding to programs to meet the needs of the parents with whom they are working. For instance, an awareness of the value systems of the parents who are being trained is important. Some parents are opposed to behavioralism; others resist democratic family decisions. Not attending to these philosophical differences can jeopardize a training program.

Some of the programs that appear in kit form are:

Systematic Training for Effective Parenting
(STEP) (1976)
    Authors: Dinkmeyer & McKay
    Source: American Guidance Service
                  Circle Pines, MN 55614

The Art of Parenting (1977)
    Authors: Wagonseller, Burnett, Salzberg, & Burnett
    Source: Research Press
                  2612 N. Mattis Ave.
                  Champaign, IL 61820

Managing Behavior (1974)
    Author: McDowell
    Source: Research Press
                  2612 N. Mattis Ave.
                  Champaign, IL 61820

Teaching Involved Parenting (TIP) (1982)
    Authors: Wagonseller & McDowell
    Source: Research Press
                  2612 N. Mattis Ave.
                  Champaign, IL 61820

Other well-defined programs that are not in kit form, such as *Assertive Discipline* (Canter & Canter, 1982), are attractive to parents and trainers.

One obviously will want to review materials carefully before using them. A good knowledge of the parents will help the leader match examples in the program to parents in the group. The leader's guide in any of the programs can be useful with any type of group.

SUMMARY

Parent training groups have become a popular means of working with parents of exceptional children. Strategies for training parents to become therapists for their own children are formulated around all the major theoretical positions, and they all report successful results.

These training efforts represent a Level 3 Need in the Mirror Model. Parents with the time, strength, energy, ability, and desire may want to learn to conduct these groups, and they can be a definite asset to a comprehensive parent involvement program. These parents are then participating at a Level 4 Strengths position in the Mirror Model, by taking leadership roles. Only an estimated 20% or so of the total parent population is ready and able to participate in a parent training group at a given time. The rest of the parents are *not* bad, uncaring parents just because they do not volunteer for or agree to parent training sessions.

One advantage to parent training groups is that they appear to use the leader's time more effectively than does individual training. Also, parents in groups discover that they are not alone in their feelings, and they realize that they can learn from each other.

Controversy still exists over whether teachers should conduct groups for parents of children in their own classes. These meetings usually have been conducted by leaders other than the teacher, but the teacher still may want to consider the technique as one to try.

REFERENCES

Adamson, G.A. (1970). *Educational modulation center* (Final Report, E.S.E.A., P.L. 89-10, Title III). Olathe, Kansas: Unified School District No. 233.

Canter, L., & Canter, M. (1982). *Assertive discipline for parents*. Santa Monica, CA: Harper & Row.

Dinkmeyer, D., & Carlson, J. (Eds.). (1973). *Consulting: Facilitating human potential and change processes*. Columbus, OH: Charles E. Merrill.

Gordon, T. *Parent effectiveness training*. (1970). New York: Peter H. Wyden.

Guerney, B.R., Jr. (Ed.) (1969). *Psychotherapeutic agents: New roles for nonprofessionals*. New York: Holt, Rinehart & Winston.

Keppers, G.L., & Caplan, S.W. (1962). Group counseling with academically able underachieving students. *New Mexico Social Studies Education Research Bulletin, 12*, 17-28.

McCowan, R.J. (1968). Group counseling with underachievers and their parents. *School Counselor, 16*, 30-35.

Thorne, F.C. (1962). Principles of directive counseling and psychotherapy. In H.J. Peters et al. (Eds), *Counseling: Selected readings*. Columbus, OH: Charles E. Merrill.

ACTIVITIES

1. Read more extensively about one of the types of groups reported in this chapter and explain it to the class.

2. Discuss the pros and cons of the teacher's being the leader of a group.

3. Role play a group meeting using one of the programs outlined in this chapter.

4. Design a parent group and implement it.

Conclusion

Many teacher training programs, unfortunately, do not provide an opportunity for students to learn the skills and techniques of conferring with parents. The importance of effective parent-teacher relationships cannot be overemphasized. Teachers who understand the child in his/her home environment can make appropriate educational plans in the classroom. Parents who are provided with information about the school setting and their child's progress can be strong supporters and assistants in the child's educational growth and development. Parents and teachers who recognize each other's capabilities can join together in successful problem solving.

Since the time the original edition of this book appeared, a number of the suggestions that were presented therein became requirements of PL 94-142. Parents and teachers have begun meeting frequently for IEP conferences and staffings. The material added to this book remains consistent with the original thesis: Positive interaction between the significant adults in the child's life will lead to growth.

The Mirror Model of Parental Involvement became a framework for trying to piece together the activities that encompass a comprehensive parent involvement program. It was conceptualized to help the reader remember that parents of exceptional children are not a homogeneous group and that programs to involve them must be individualized, just as we individualize for children.

Over the years, we have become increasingly aware of the need to recognize the selectiveness of perceptions and the part values play in understanding oneself and others. Teachers who have never had a handicapped child cannot walk in the shoes of a parent who has a handicapped child, but they can cultivate a sensitivity to the dynamics of the life of the family and in that way become more understanding.

CLAIMING THE CHILD

A good teacher once said that until teachers "claimed" a child as their own responsibility or the parents "claimed" the child as a part of their life, the child's chances for growth were nil. By this she meant that teachers must care for children to the extent that they will go beyond the brief interactions that occur in subject matter presentations. It does not mean that teachers should try to "own" a child and the child's problems, but that they feel strongly enough about the child's welfare that they will provide many opportunities for children to grow and allow them to accept responsibility for their own behavior. Teachers show that they care by verbal and nonverbal clues.

Many teachers show they care for the children in their classroom by sharing in the joys and important events in each child's life. Some teachers send their pupils birthday cards, Christmas cards, and valentine cards through the mail. Everyone enjoys receiving mail, and a personally addressed card from the teacher is especially appreciated. Some teachers phone the child when they see something they think the pupil would be interested in, or they call the parents when something "neat" has happened to the child that day in the classroom. These little touches help the child know that he/she has been "claimed" by the teacher and has entered into the teacher's world.

REINFORCING THE PARENTS

A part of really entering into the child's world is to realize that the other significant adults in the child's life need reinforcement for their good work. On the one hand, providing reinforcement is good public relations; on the other hand, if the parents have entered into a project to help solve a problem, reinforcing them is necessary to the success of the project. Nielsen (1972) found that when an academic or social problem was identified and reported to the parents, the children whose parents were reinforced for working with their children grew significantly more than those whose parents were not reinforced. In fact, to present parents with information that their child was having academic and social problems and not to provide the parents with tasks to help their children and reinforcement for carrying out the tasks was often detrimental to the child's growth.

For parents to change set patterns of behavior is difficult. Therefore, when parents are asked to alter their daily lives by listening to their child read, play games, or make class projects, the parents seem to fulfill these tasks more readily if the teacher shows approval through words of praise, notes, letters, and telephone calls. The more positive the interaction between parents and teachers, the higher is the probability that both parents and teachers will work in the best interests of the child.

TIMING THE CONFERENCES

The teacher must consider the effects on the child of the timing of conferences. As Duncan and Fitzgerald (1969) pointed out, conferences held before school starts seem to be in the child's best interests. Kroth (1972) stated that conferences held on a regularly scheduled basis, and particularly when the child is performing well, appear to facilitate appropriate behavior. Adhering to time limits and setting termination dates for the number of conferences seems to have the effect of increasing parents' effectiveness in problem solving (Barten & Barten, 1973). Therefore, when using a conference as a technique for helping the child, the teacher who has "claimed" the child will carefully consider when to hold a conference, how long the conferences should be, and whether to set a tentative limit on the number of conferences.

Sometimes, because of institutional requirements, the teacher cannot control the length of conferences. The teacher, however, can do several things to help the flow of the interaction. Giving parents "tip sheets" (see Appendix B) in advance, preparing an agenda, and paying careful attention to the conference environment will facilitate the meeting. Parents should be apprised of how long each conference is expected to take. Openness and sharing of information will make a major difference in contacts between parents and teachers.

DEMONSTRATING TO PARENTS

Sometimes parents do not understand directions the teacher gives. Then the procedures outlined in the conference, which were meant to be positive, become negative. Many group parent programs (see chapter 12) employ demonstrations as part of their teaching techniques. If the clarity of the procedure or whether the parent can carry out the technique is questionable, demonstrating the procedures for the parents may be wise. Many times we learn best by imitation or by modeling after a master teacher. Teachers should not hesitate to *show* parents the techniques they think may be effective.

At one time teachers told parents not to try to teach their own child to read, spell, or do other types of academic work. The feeling was that the parents would put too much pressure on the child and cause more problems than were solved. Many professionals have come to the realization that they cannot do the entire job alone, that parents are teachers, and that sharing with parents the techniques teachers have found to be effective with children may be to the child's benefit. Dentists teach children how to take care of their teeth; physical therapists show parents how to exercise their children; psychologists teach parents to be therapists for their own children. In fact, almost every helping profession has considered techniques for instructing parents to share in the practice of their skills.

Special educators have also begun to use this strategy in the best interests of their pupils. Preschool programs for the deaf, blind, and physically handicapped have strong parent components. This part of their programs has not been by chance. There are not enough professionals to provide all handicapped children with the services they need; and even if there were, it would not negate the importance of parents as teachers of their own child.

Something about a relationship between a parent and teacher that is built on respect makes both individuals more capable of serving children in their own best interests. The only thing lacking in many teachers is the confidence to take the first step.

If you've "claimed" a child and want to share something "whippy" the child did today, put down this book and pick up the phone. Call someone else who cares as much as you do and who will be equally excited—the child's parents!

REFERENCES

Barten, H.H., & Barten, S.S. (1973). *Children and their parents in brief therapy.* New York: Behavioral Publications.

Duncan, L.W., & Fitzgerald, P.W. (1969) Increasing the parent-child communication through counselor-parent conferences. *Personnel & Guidance Journal,* pp. 514-517.

Kroth, R. (1972). Facilitating educational progress by improving parent conferences. *Focus on Exceptional Children, 4*(7), 1-10.

Nielsen, R.R. (1972). *The influence of reinforced parents on behaviorally disturbed children.* Unpublished master's thesis, University of Kansas, Lawrence.

ACTIVITIES

1. Have your principal take a picture of you and a parent and a child who have worked together successfully. Put it in your billfold and ...

2. Call another parent!

Appendix A
**Case Histories for
Role Playing Exercises
(page 79)**

CASE HISTORY #1

Present Status

Billy is a 10-year-old white male whose mother is requesting placement and who has been evaluated and recommended for placement in an intermediate class for the emotionally disturbed. The family has just moved from K., where Billy was in a regular third-grade class. His teacher was Mrs. Dropshot, who is now in a psychiatric ward at the State Hospital.

Physical Appearance

The child was not present for the conference, so this information is from the mother's report: "He's just all boy... He's very active—can climb to the roof of the school in Louisburg even though he does not have a right arm... He doesn't sleep well at nights and is still a bed-wetter occasionally."

Educational Status

Billy has been in four different schools since he started 5 years ago. As a Navy man, his father traveled around. billy failed first and third grades. A psychologist said he had normal ability to learn.

Personal Traits

He doesn't get along too well with the kids in the neighborhood. He'd rather hunt, fish, or watch TV. He never misses "Dukes of Hazzard" or "Night Rider." "His favorite food is peanut butter and banana sandwiches. He wants to be a Navy man like his Dad, who is a no-good bum."

Home and Family

The family has five children. The two girls are the father's, two boys are the mother's, and Billy is a product of both mother and father. Billy gets along best with the older girl, who is in the 10th grade.

The probation officer sees a ninth-grade stepbrother once a month. The Johnson County Mental Health Center says that the mother and father need to be more interested in what the children are doing, "but how can we when we have so many kids?"

"Billy likes dogs, but last summer he put kerosene on a cat and lit it on fire. He says he doesn't know why he did it. He's usually pretty good with animals. When his dad got back from his 2-week tour of duty in Bethesda, Maryland, he really tanned him for that."

TEST: CASE #1

1. What is the child's name?

2. How old is he?

3. Has he been in special education before?

4. How many children are in the family?

5. Does the child have any physical problems? If so, what?

6. Has school been a successful experience for the child? Why do you draw the conclusion you have?

7. Has the child or family had contact with any social agencies? If so, which ones?

8. What might be good reinforcers for him?

9. Does the child have any unusual personality traits?

10. From whom would you like reports? Why?

CASE HISTORY #2

For Regular Class Teacher

Present Status

Suzie is an 8-year-old girl. Her mother moved to O. from R., California, where Suzie was enrolled in the third grade. The mother has taken a job as counselor in a nearby junior college. The father has remained in California with his car wash business.

Physical Appearance

Because of her poor vision, Suzie can barely see to put the batteries in her hearing aid. He mother has an appointment with an ophthalmologist next month because the school nurse believes that Suzie's vision can be corrected with glasses. Suzie has had perfect attendance at school ever since she started first grade.

Educational Status

Suzie has been in the low reading group and low math group. She was in a summer remedial reading program, which the mother felt was of questionable value. The girl always tries hard to complete her tasks and often cries if she cannot get finished. Her teachers have always gotten along well with Suzie, and the mother feels that her daughter might have received "social promotions" in school. The mother doesn't know what books the California schools used with her.

Suzie's achievement test scores consistently have been in the 10-15 percentile. She has never had an individual evaluation by a psychologist.

Personal Traits

Though fairly quiet, Suzie seems to get along with other children. Most of her friends are 2 or 3 years younger. She likes to play house, Four Square, Mother May I, and other games. She watches TV, but she sits so close and turns it up so loud that the mother discourages TV watching. She likes to fingerpaint, but it's pretty messy.

Since moving to O., she doesn't like being in her room alone at night. There is no particular food that she likes or dislikes.

Home and Family

Suzie is an only child. The parents are at least temporarily separated; whether the separation will become legal is still speculative. Family income is modest but adequate. Suzie is cooperative at home and is somewhat of a "mama's girl."

Additional Information

Her mother feels that Suzie needs additional individual testing and wonders if repeating the third grade might be a good idea.

TEST: CASE #2

1. How old is the child?

2. Does she have any physical problems that will require special teacher attention? If so, what?

3. How is the child's general health?

4. What books were used with her in the previous school?

5. From where did she move?

6. Was the child a good, average, or poor student?

7. Does she get along with other children? Teachers?

8. Who is her favorite brother or sister?

9. What reinforcers are available in the home?

10. What personality problems should the teacher be concerned with?

CASE HISTORY #3

Present Status

Ricky is 6 years old. His father is a migrant worker who was born in Mexico and is applying for citizenship this year. His mother is a Native American. The family lives in a trailer court on the outskirts of C.

Physical Appearance

A handsome boy, Ricky has big brown eyes that have a sort of sad look. His mother reports that he is no trouble around home and that he doesn't talk much. In fact, his only speech usually revolves around something he wants or needs. He is a very slight child who tries to fade into the background whenever possible. He has had a lot of colds and earaches but has never been to a doctor.

Educational Status

Because of the itinerant nature of his father's job, Ricky's family moved several times last year. Some of the school systems did not have a kindergarten, but he attended school regularly when a class was available. He can print his name and recognize the letters in it, but he does not know other letters consistently. His mother has tried to teach him to write numbers, but he hasn't seemed very interested. As far as the mother knows, he has taken no standardized tests. She has never had a conference with any of his teachers before, and Ricky has never expressed an opinion about any of his teachers.

Personal Traits

Ricky doesn't like to play much with other children, though he gets along with them. He prefers to draw, which is something he does a lot—covering everything from brown paper grocery sacks to newspaper margins with miniature people. These drawings are very detailed. His mother, who is proud of her son's products, has a sample drawing in her purse. She thinks Ricky may turn out to be an artist. The family has a television set, but it has been broken for some time.

Home and Family

Ricky's father was tired of moving around, so he found a job as a stocker in a supermarket and hopes to live here permanently. Besides Ricky, the family has two other children—a boy 4 years old and a baby girl. Ricky likes to care for the baby, but he tends to ignore his brother, an active child who spends much time playing outside with a gang of his friends. Ricky is a big help to his mother; he likes to do all kinds of chores. These mostly involve running errands and helping her clean. He doesn't do very much with his father, who is not inclined to spend time with him anyway, preferring to take Ricky's little brother with him when he goes fishing. English is the only language spoken in the home, and the father is quite proficient at it.

TEST: CASE #3

1. What is the child's ancestry?

2. How old is he?

3. Does he have any physical problems that may need attention? If so, what?

4. Does he have any unusual personality traits with which the teacher should be concerned?

5. How many children are in the family?

6. What are the child's social relationships?

7. What reinforcers are available in the home?

8. What is the family's socioeconomic status?

9. Is it likely that the child has previously experienced academic success?

10. Are there any unusual circumstances in the child's family life?

CASE HISTORY #4

Present Status

Jay is a 7-year-old white male who has not attended school before, except for a short period in a special class in a closed psychiatric ward in a Detroit hospital. He was evaluated there, and residential placement was recommended at that time, nearly 1 year ago. Since then his mother has married and moved to S. She now wants Jay to attend a public school, possibly in a special class, though she isn't sure.

Physical Appearance

For his age, Jay is large and also strong physically. His mother has had quite a bit of trouble controlling his temper outbursts and lately has given up trying. She thinks Jay is just unusually stubborn. His new stepfather has had a little more success in discipline attempts, but it's still too early to say whether he will be effective in this. In addition to his aggressive behavior, Jay seems to be a nervous child and stutters considerably, though usually with just the initial word in a sentence.

Educational Status

The boy has had little or no exposure to academic work, either formally or informally. He has never really attended school, and his mother thinks he would not pay attention to anything she tried to teach him. Jay has no concept of numbers or letters even though these were introduced briefly during his short stay in the hospital school. His records during this hospitalization may be available, but the mother has never seen them. She thinks they tested him extensively.

Personal Traits

Jay doesn't play much with children his own age. He is destructive of other kids' property, and after he destroys a toy or two, they won't play with him anymore. He also has torn up most of his own belongings and other things in the home that were not under lock and key. He likes to play with matches and lighters, so these must be kept from him. He likes all kinds of food and will eat almost anything available, including bugs.

Home and Family

Jay is an only child. His father's whereabouts are unknown; and he was never married to Jay's mother, having left town soon after finding out she was pregnant. From the time Jay was 2 years old, his mother worked as a waitress and dancer in a bar until recently, when she married for the first time. Since she worked nights, she slept most of the day and left Jay to his own devices. She feels guilty about this and now feels that "things will be different" and wants to "start over with Jay."

On two separate occasions firemen put out fires Jay had started in an old garage behind his apartment building, and they took him to the hospital. After being called for the second time within a month, they took him to the hospital's psychiatric receiving center. Jay's mother feels responsible for his behavior since he had little or no supervision from her. She believes that now that she won't be working, "things will get straightened out."

Jay's new stepfather is a pharmaceutical salesman who was recently transferred to this area. His sales territory is large (three states). He was married once before but has no children of his own. Both parents emphatically do not want residential placement for Jay.

TEST: CASE #4

1. What is the child's age?

2. How many other children are in the home?

3. Does the child have any physical problems? If so, what?

4. Has contact been made with any social agencies? If so, which ones?

5. Does he have any unusual personality traits?

6. Would you like to see any of his previous records? If so, which ones?

7. What possible reinforcers could be used in the classroom or at home?

8. Would you advise special class placement? Why or why not?

9. Have the child's interpersonal relationships been satisfactory?

Appendix B
Tip Sheets

Parent Tips for School Conferences

A parent-teacher conference is a chance for two very important adults to talk about how a child is doing in school. It is a time for you, as a parent, to ask questions about any concerns you may have about your child's progress. Since the time allowed for conferences is often limited, it is helpful for both parents and teachers to plan ahead.

Here is a checklist that may help you get ready for your conference.

HOW TO GET READY

_____ 1. Make a list of questions and concerns.

_____ 2. Ask your child if he/she has questions for the teacher.

_____ 3. Arrange for a babysitter for small children.

QUESTIONS YOU MAY WANT TO ASK

_____ 1. In which subjects does my child do well? Is my child having any trouble?

_____ 2. Does my child get along with other children?

_____ 3. Does my child obey the teacher?

_____ 4. How can I help at home?

QUESTIONS THE TEACHER MAY ASK YOU

_____ 1. What does your child like best about school?

_____ 2. What does your child do after school? (What are his/her interests?)

_____ 3. Does your child have time and space set aside for homework?

_____ 4. How is your child's health?

_____ 5. Are there any problems that may affect your child's learning?

_____ 6. What type of discipline works well at home?

AT THE CONFERENCE

_____ 1. Please arrive on time.

_____ 2. Discuss your questions and concerns.

_____ 3. Share information that will help the teacher know your child better.

_____ 4. Take notes if you wish.

AFTER THE CONFERENCE

_____ 1. If you have more questions or you ran out of time, make another appointment.

_____ 2. Tell your child about the conference.

_____ 3. Plan to keep in touch with the teacher.

_____ 4. If you were satisfied with the conference, write a note to the teacher.

Developed by the Parent Center, Albuquerque, NM

Tips for Parents
On Being an Active Participant

In these days of "my *rights*," parents and children, as well as schools, also have *responsibilities*. A major responsibility is to become an active, cooperative, contributing member of the child's educational program. Here are some suggestions that may help.

General

1. You are the major, and perhaps only, coordinator of all your child's records. Keep a file on educational, psychological, and medical records.
2. Initiate a conference prior to or early in the school year, if one has not been initiated by school personnel. Indicate persons you would like to be present.
3. Join parent organizations such as PTA or parent advisory groups—or help start one if none is available.
4. Attend school board meetings, parent group meetings, parent advisory committees, and lend your support to quality education programs.
5. Write notes and letters and make phone calls reinforcing even small accomplishments by teachers, administrators, and school board members. Remember that they are trying! Since most of the communication they receive is critical, they appreciate when people recognize the good as well as the not-so-good.

Pre-Conference

1. Review records and notes on past conferences.
2. Hold a pre-conference meeting with your mate and child to determine questions to ask and information to share.
3. Write down a list of questions you want to ask.
4. Write down information you would like the teacher to be aware of.
5. Write down suggestions you have for your child's program.
6. If you feel uneasy about the conference, invite your mate, a friend, or another parent to go with you. A second person often can help you ask questions and can be helpful after the conference in discussing what was said.
7. Collect whatever records you think you will need, plus a pencil and paper.
8. Check the time of the conference.

Conference

1. Be on time.
2. Find out how much time has been allowed for the meeting. It will help you pace yourself.
3. Introduce yourself and anybody you have brought along. Be friendly and try to put the school people at ease. Remember, you are here to help plan your child's program — not to do battle.

Being an Active Participant (cont.)

4. If a number of people are present, sit in the middle instead of at the end. This indicates that you plan to be an active working member of the group and not just a recipient.
5. Take notes during the meeting, particularly on those items that school personnel say will be done or will not be done and those things you agree to do.
6. Ask for clarification on anything you do not understand. Knowledgeable people should be able to explain jargon or specialized terms clearly.
7. Ask to see any records that you want, and have them explained to your satisfaction.
8. Remain cool and cooperative to the greatest extent possible.
9. At the end of the conference, if the school personnel do not summarize, do it for them. Indicate who is to do what.
10. If the conference time runs out and you do not feel that you are finished, arrange for another conference.
11. Sign only those papers you are sure you understand clearly.
12. Above all, try to be supportive. Try not to put the teacher on the defensive. The teacher and other school people may have had many conferences that day, most of which were as complex as yours. The teacher really appreciates parents who help develop meaningful programs in positive ways.

Post-Conference

1. Check your notes. See if it is clear as to what you are to do and what the school personnel are supposed to do. If you have taken a friend or another parent, check for agreement in perceptions.
2. Share information with your mate and child.
3. Send the school personnel a letter thanking them for their efforts if you think it is justified.

CHILDREN BENEFIT THE MOST WHEN THERE IS *ACTIVE* AND *COOPERATIVE* PARTICIPATION BY PARENTS AND SCHOOL PERSONNEL.

Developed by Roger Kroth

Tips for Parents:
Spending Quality Time with Your Children

1. Plan for quality time. It doesn't just "happen."

2. Develop shared interests with each child.

3. Practice good listening skills.

4. Be willing to change your agenda occasionally to attend to your child's.

5. Be accepting of your child's feelings. You don't have to agree or encourage—just accept.

6. Try to be consistent and trustworthy by following through on plans. Make special time a regular occurrence.

7. Emphasize the positive. Try to convey the message that your child is loved unconditionally.

8. Enjoy your child and yourself. Have fun together!

Developed by the Parent Center, Albuquerque, NM

Tips for "Street-Proofing" Your Child

1. Teach your child what a *stranger* is. Most children think at first that a stranger is someone who acts strange.
2. Teach your child not to take rides, candy, money, or bribes from a stranger. Often children are bribed into being helpful or accepting help. A lost dog, kitten, or toy may be used as bait.
3. Teach your child never to accept an alternative way home. Children need to know that any change in plans will be relayed to them only through school personnel.
4. Teach your child that he/she has a private space that has to be respected by strangers.
5. Teach your child that any area covered by a bathing suit or underwear should not be touched by strangers.
6. Don't allow children to break the rules in your presence. Don't allow strangers to give them candy or ruffle their hair even when you are with them.
7. Provide "safe places" for your children on their way home. Show them places they can go if they need help, such as a neighbor's home or a certain store, to use the telephone.
8. Teach your child things to do if approached by a stranger, such as: ignoring, walking away, using the "safe places" in the neighborhood or, if approached by someone in a car, heading the opposite direction.
9. Encourage your child to tell you if he/she has encountered a situation that makes him/her uncomfortable.
10. Practice and repeat these tips so that your child will form good safety habits. Review them and role play possible situations at regular intervals.

Adapted from remarks by Dr. Marian Shelton

Survival Tips for Parents

1. Be realistic about what your child can do.

2. Recognize that you make the rules in your home.

3. Model the kind of behavior you'd like to see in your children. Examples speak louder than words.

4. Discipline clearly.

   - Be short and to the point without lecturing, nagging, or using put-downs.
   - Don't give children too much room for discussion.
   - When you know you're right, why argue?
   - Compromise when necessary.

5. Deal with problems as they occur.

6. Use "Grandma's Rule": Work before play.

7. Present a consistent, united front.

8. Establish a daily study hall/quiet time Sunday through Thursday.

9. Assign chores with allowance dependent upon their completion.

10. Be aware of your children's social activities; know their friends, where they're going, time of return.

11. Establish and maintain physical and emotional closeness.

12. Keep in touch with your child's teacher/school.

13. Work together and play together.

Adapted from comments by Dr. Tom Carey

Tips for Parents of Children
With Learning Disabilities

1. Try to find out specifically what your child's learning disability is and understand how it affects his/her daily living.

2. Ask for help from people who know your child's problem:

    • Teacher
    • Counselor
    • Diagnostician
    • Doctor.

3. Decide on the behavioral expectations you have for your learning disabled child.

4. Tell the child what behavior you expect and the consequences for noncompliance.

5. Step in the first time the child misbehaves, and do not make idle threats.

6. Try to carry out consequences without long lectures.

7. Really listen to your child. When the child misbehaves, he/she often is saying "help me."

8. Work toward accepting your child as he/she is.

    • Try not to "fix" your child.
    • Teach your child in a way he/she can learn; for example, ask or tell the child one thing at a time.

9. Let up on the pressure, and spend positive, quality time with your child.

10. Give praise for the smallest accomplishment.

11. Find your child's strong points and praise him/her for things well done. Try not to dwell on the failures.

12. Help other children in the family, and adults, accept this child. Don't let them make fun of him/her or what the child is doing to learn.

13. Try to anticipate your child's needs. Don't put him/her in a group that would do more harm than good.

14. Work toward developing "long patience" and understanding.

    • Give short-term jobs, one at a time.
    • Adjust family living to give this child the time he/she needs.

Tips — Learning Disabled (cont.)

15. Try to be honest with your child.

    - Don't say, "There's nothing wrong with you"; No one knows better than the child does that something *is* wrong with his/her learning process.
    - Try to explain the problem to the child with ways to cope.
    - Don't promise a quick cure.

16. Take a positive approach.

    - There is help.
    - These children can learn with special help.

17. Try to develop faith and trust in the people who are trying to help your child; give qualified suggestions a chance.

18. Keep communication lines open between parent, child, and teacher at all times.

19. Check out anything you're not sure about. Try to understand all you can.

20. Talk with other parents who have children in learning disability classes.

Adapted from *Counseling Parents of Exceptional Children* by J.C. Stewart, 1978, Columbus, OH: Charles E. Merrill

Tips for Parents of a Gifted Child

1. Remember that each gifted child is a unique individual rooted in a certain family, community, and culture. Gifted children cannot be stereotyped. Certain general principles apply to their guidance, but gifted children all differ from each other.

2. Try to realize that gifted children are, first of all, children. They need:

    - Love, but controls.
    - Attention, but discipline.
    - Parent involvement, yet training in self-dependence and responsibility.

3. Respect your child and his/her knowledge, which at times may be better than your own. Gifted children sometimes are impatient with authority.

    - Assume that the child means to do right.
    - Allow as much liberty as you can on unimportant issues.
    - Try to give general instructions to carry out in his/her own creative way rather than specific commands to carry out in yours.
    - Provide clear expectations for behavior.

4. Talk with your child about the importance of conventions such as politeness, manners, courtesy, and regard for others. A gifted child's impatience with conventions may cause problems.

5. Discuss disciplinary actions. Gifted children seem to understand rational arguments and usually have a well-developed sense of duty.

6. Try to set as few limits as are really necessary, but when you set them, be sure to follow through. Gifted children are particularly curious to see if you will be consistent. Gifted children, however, may need fewer constraints than others.

7. Encourage your child to participate in developing limits for himself/herself. Since gifted children are highly verbal, they tend to argue and to logically defend their reasoning and viewpoint. Try to see this as a strength to be put to good use in establishing limits rather than as a threat to enforcement.

8. Allow your child to *choose* in as many situations as possible. Gifted children need choices and thrive on them. Make sure, though, that the choices are agreeable to *you.*

9. Try to respond to your child's needs, not to his/her negative behavior. Understanding the child's needs, however, does not mean that you must accept or even tolerate his/her behavior.

10. Convey trust that your child will act wisely.

11. Take time to be with your child, listen to what he/she has to say, and discuss ideas with him/her. Be a good example yourself.

12. Emphasize early verbal expression, reading, discussing ideas, poetry, and music.

13. Read to your child. Provide good books, magazines, and other media.

14. Emphasize doing well in school.

15. Encourage your child's questions, but insist that he/she not ask them at inappropriate times.

    • When needed, have the child sharpen or rephrase his/her questions to clarify them.
    • Occasionally reply to a question with a question that will send the child searching in larger directions.
    • When you cannot answer a question, direct the child to a resource who can.

16. Stimulate and widen your child's mind through suitable experiences with books, recreation, travel, and the arts.

17. Encourage the child to follow through on things and strive for real mastery rather than "going through" a lot of hobbies or collections in a short time. Gifted children usually have a wide, versatile range of interests but may have problems concentrating in one area for long.

18. Avoid overstructuring the child's life so that he/she doesn't have any free time. A child cannot be expected to perform at top capacity at all times.

19. Provide the stimulation of lessons in a special skill, an able companion with whom to spend time, and special experiences outside the home.

20. Laugh with your child; seek to develop his/her sense of humor.

Adapted from *Counseling Parents of Exceptional Children* by J.C. Stewart, 1978, Columbus, OH: Charles E. Merrill

Tips for Parenting a Gifted Child

1. Your child is a child first and gifted second. A 5-year-old may be able to solve mathematical problems worth bragging about to grandparents, but he/she has lived only 5 years. Only behavior appropriate for a 5-year-old should be expected.
2. Don't compare your gifted child to other children. That places on the gifted one the burden to live up to that image all the time, and it certainly is no fun for whoever comes off second best. All children are unique and special in their own ways.
3. Listen to your gifted child. Dinner may be about to burn, and the telephone ringing, but *listen*, because the question may be important. If ignored, the curiosity to ask may eventually disappear. The one thing all of us can give our children is our undivided attention.
4. It's a great big wonderful world! Show it to your gifted child in the form of trips, books, interesting people, symphonies, digs, museums, fire stations, wiggly things, theater, daisy chains, and the magical chemistry that makes a cake rise.
5. Let the child specialize early if he/she wants to. Living with dinosaurs from morning to night has fringe benefits. A child may be keeping notes and records, learning to do research, and discovering the Dewey Decimal System along with Tyrannosaurus.
6. A child doesn't have to be gainfully occupied every waking minute. Allow him/her time to daydream, be silly, do baby things, and lie on the unmade bed and contemplate the ceiling. Gifted children are usually creative, and being creative on schedule is difficult.
7. Praise your gifted child for his/her efforts. Give praise for the wonderful things he/she does. If the great experiment does not work or the shaky tower of blocks comes tumbling down, praise the child for trying. Inquiring minds must take intellectual risks, and risk taking requires support and praise.
8. Discipline is necessary for harmonious family life. Dinner time comes at the same time for all brothers and sisters, gifted or not. Giftedness is no excuse for unacceptable behavior.
9. Don't expect your gifted child to be gifted all the time. That kind of halo makes for bad headaches.
10. *Enjoy!* Gifted children are curious, enthusiastic, excited about new things, and able to communicate early. Relax and enjoy!

From Gina Ginsberg, Executive Director, Gifted Child Society, Inc., Oakland, NJ

Tips for Parents: Talking with Medical Personnel

1. Ask doctors, nurses, and others any questions you have about your child's health and care. Also ask them for clarification if you don't understand their jargon.

2. If you want to ask sensitive questions and your child or other people are present, ask to speak to medical personnel in private if it will make you feel more comfortable.

3. Keep in mind your right to ask questions. If you have many complex questions, however, you may wish to arrange a separate appointment when more time will be available to discuss them in detail.

4. Bring out, and ask professionals to bring out, any positive progress your child has made. This can be helpful to you and your child. Medical situations are often oriented toward problems. Sometimes progress and development tend not to be emphasized.

5. Ask, if you don't know, what the next logical areas for change and progress might be.

6. Find someone involved with your child's care whom you respect and can talk to; knowledge as well as personality is important.

7. Consider asking all of your child's specialists to meet together with you at some point to discuss progress, future goals, and plans.

8. Search for information:

   - Read anything you can find on the topic.
   - Write to anyone who has information.
   - Ask those who work with your child if they know of any relevant articles that could help you understand your child's disability.

9. Between visits, make a list of questions that occur to you; sometimes they are hard to remember later.

10. Make a list of any questions your child may have. This is one good way to reinforce your child's role in his/her own care.

Adapted from the *ACLD Newsletter*, January/February, 1983. The list was originally compiled by Betty Anderson, Federation for Children with Special Needs. Suite 338. 120 Boylston St., Boston, MA, and first published in the *SLD Gazette*.

198

Tips for Parents: Discipline

1. Love your child even when you are unhappy with his/her behavior.

2. Know how you want your child to behave, and tell him/her what you expect.

3. Make rules clear and simple. Tell your child ahead of time what the rules are.

4. Know what can be expected of children at certain ages. Try not to give your child more responsibility than he/she can handle.

5. Set an example for your child. Children learn from watching others, especially their parents.

6. Catch your child being good and make sure he/she knows you have noticed. For example, smile, tell the child you are pleased with his/her behavior, give hugs, etc.

7. Be consistent when you discipline your child so he/she knows what to expect.

8. If you don't like some of your child's behaviors, remember that you can't change everything at once. Try to change only one behavior at a time.

9. Whenever you can, praise your child for behaving the way you want him her to.

10. Expect your child to behave, and most times he/she will.

Developed by the Parent Center, Albuquerque, NM

Tips for Dealing with Aggression

DO . . .

- Listen.
- Write down what they say.
- When they slow down, ask them what else is bothering them.
- Exhaust their list of complaints.
- Ask them to clarify any specific complaints that are too general.
- Show them the list and ask if it is complete.
- Ask them for suggestions for solving any of the problems they've listed.
- Write down the suggestions.
- As much as possible, mirror their body posture during this process.
- As they speak louder, speak softer.

DON'T . . .

- Argue.
- Defend or become defensive.
- Promise things you can't produce.
- Own problems that belong to others.
- Raise your voice.
- Belittle or minimize the problem.

Developed by the Parent Center, Albuquerque, NM

Tips for Parents: Typical Adolescent Behavior

- Strengthening self-identity.

- Concern with physical changes.

- Confusion about the desire for independence vs. dependence.

- Mood swings; quick changes of feelings.

- Not confiding, talking over problems, discussing feelings or ideas.

- Impulsive behavior.

- A need to not be with the family.

- Anxiety about growing up.

- Influence of, and devotion to, peer group.

- Conflict with parents.

Developed by the Parent Center, Albuquerque, NM

Tips for Parents: Helping Children
Feel Good About Themselves

Children view themselves by the way they think other people who are important in their lives feel about them. We, as parents and teachers, must make sure we are doing all we can to help children feel good about themselves.

1. Treat children with respect, and expect the same behavior from them.

2. Help children find their strengths; they know their weaknesses.

3. Encourage children in areas of both strengths and weaknesses.

4. Find ways to recognize each child as special. Try to avoid comparing one child to another.

5. Try to listen to children and understand their points of view.

6. Encourage children to express feelings, both good and bad, without fear of losing your love.

7. When you are displeased with something children have done, discipline them for a specific behavior, which is clear to them, and not because they are "bad."

8. Help children discover acceptable ways to behave in areas where they are having difficulty.

9. Let children know you have confidence in them by giving them ways to be successfully independent.

10. Hug and praise children at every opportunity.

Children model many adult behaviors. They will notice if you feel good about *yourself* and *your* place in the world. Therefore, we need to work on building our own self-esteem as well as that of our children.

Developed by the Parent Center, Albuquerque, NM

Tips for Parents: Helping Your Child Do Well in School

Building Good Study Habits

1. Provide a quiet work place.

2. Build in a set time for study every day. Right after school or after dinner are good times.

3. Keep the study time even if the child doesn't have homework. That time can be spent reading, doing math, or something you assign. (Many times students are rewarded with free time when they don't bring their work home. This builds poor study habits.)

4. Begin by setting 20 to 30 minutes of study time, depending on the age of the child. If more time is needed, add it gradually.

5. If the child is having trouble getting started with homework, help with the first problem or give an example.

6. If the child wastes study time, set limits on how long he/she has to complete a task.

7. Work *before* play is still a good rule.

8. Check with your child's teacher to see what school work is to be done.

9. Praise and rewards tell the child he/she is being successful.

10. *Consistency* is the key word in building a habit.

Parent-Child Learning Activities

1. Read *with* your child 20 to 30 minutes each day or several times a week. Often, if a parent and child trade off reading paragraphs or pages, the child will get less tired and stay interested in the story.

2. Read *to* your child. Children can understand and enjoy material they cannot read by themselves.

3. Have your child read *alone* 15 or 20 minutes each day, or more if he/she wants to. Make a graph charting minutes of reading each day. The

child can do the charting. Build in rewards for x number of minutes of reading each week. Rewards might be money, a movie, extra TV, special times with parent, etc.

4. Take your child to the public library to check out books.

5. Make sure that your child sees *you* reading.

6. Discuss things that are happening in the news or what the child is doing in school. This might be done during meal times.

7. Take your child on short trips around the city or state. This will help your child grow in knowledge and experience.

8. Play games with your child. Games can help children learn to think, and they give you a chance to spend some fun time together.

9. Be realistic about what you expect.

10. Remember that praise can accomplish more than punishment. Successful experiences lead to more success.

Developed by the Parent Center, Albuquerque, NM

99 WAYS TO SAY "VERY GOOD!"

1. You've got it made.
2. That's right.
3. You're on the right track now!
4. That's good!
5. You're very good at that.
6. That's coming along very nicely.
7. That's very much better!
8. Good work.
9. You're doing a good job.
10. You've just about got it!
11. That's it!
12. Congratulations!
13. I knew you could do it.
14. That's quite an improvement.
15. Now you've figured it out.
16. Now you have it.
17. Not bad.
18. Great!
19. You're learning fast.
20. Good for you!
21. You make it look easy.
22. You really make my job fun.
23. That's the right way to do it.
24. You're getting better every day.
25. You did it that time!
26. That's not half bad!
27. Wow!
28. That's the way!
29. Nice going.
30. Now you've figured it out.
31. Sensational!
32. You haven't missed a thing.
33. That's the way to do it.
34. Keep up the good work.
35. That's better.
36. Nothing can stop you now!
37. That's first-class work.
38. Excellent!
39. Perfect!
40. That's the best ever.
41. You're really going to town.
42. Fine!
43. Terrific!
44. That's better than ever.
45. You did very well on that.
46. Outstanding!
47. You did very well.
48. You're really improving.
49. Right on!
50. Good remembering!
51. I'm happy you're working like that.
52. You've about mastered that.
53. You're working hard today.
54. I'm proud of the way you worked.
55. That's the best you've ever done.
56. You're doing a lot better.
57. Keep working—you're good.
58. I couldn't have done it better.
59. That's a fine job.
60. You've been practicing!
61. You're doing beautifully.
62. Superb!
63. Keep it up!
64. You did a lot of work.
65. You've got that down pat!
66. You did well today.
67. Tremendous!
68. You're doing fine.
69. Good thinking!
70. You're learning a lot.
71. Keep trying!
72. You outdid yourself!
73. I've never seen it done better.
74. Good for you!
75. Good going!
76. I like that.
77. One more time and you'll have it.
78. I'm very proud of you.
79. That a way!
80. I think you've got it.
81. Good job, (student's name).
82. You figured that out fast.
83. You remembered.
84. That's really nice.
85. It's a pleasure to teach you.
86. You're right.
87. Clever!
88. That makes me feel good.
89. That's really great!
90. Way to go.
91. Well, look at you go!
92. Now you've got it!

93. Top notch work!
94. Your brain is in gear today!
95. Much better!
96. Wonderful!

97. Super!
98. Marvelous!
99. Wowee!

Adapted from the Illinois *ACLD*

Tips for Students:
Building Good Study Habits

Getting Ready

1. Start with *positive thinking*. You can do it if you want to.

2. Know what you have to get finished. Set goals for yourself.

3. Know yourself — when and how you work best.

    WHERE? Somewhere quiet is best. Organize your work space. Be sure you have good lighting and the materials you need to complete the assignment. If home is too crowded or noisy, ask your mom's or dad's help to find another place.

    WHEN? Ask yourself these questions: Do I work best before or after meals? Do I work best in the morning, afternoon, or evening? Set a study schedule for the time you have the most energy. This will help you finish more quickly.

    HOW? Beware of distractions. Radios, TVs, and tape recorders should be turned off or turned down *low*.

    Unexpected company can keep you from getting your work done. Ask friends to come back at another time.

    Let someone else answer the telephone and take messages. You can return calls later when you're finished.

4. Make a study schedule. It can save you time and energy and keep you from forgetting important things or from constantly having to decide what to do next.

5. Fit in the four health essentials; they will help you get good results from your studies: Schedule time every day to *exercise*, get plenty of *rest*, eat *balanced meals*, and have *fun*.

Digging In

1. Study your text, expecially the table of contents, to get an *overview* of your subject. Before each chapter, look over the main ideas, which are usually printed in heavier ink than the rest of the book.

    Find another book on the same subject in the school library, especially a book written for younger readers. You will find that the main ideas are stressed even more than in your own book. Don't bother reading every page. What you want is a general idea.

2. Be selective when *underlining*. Use your brain more than your pencil.

Building Good Study Habits (cont.)

3. Pick out *key words, dates, definitions,* and *names* to underline. If a section seems important to you, draw a vertical line next to it in the margin. Words such as *because, in addition, later, also, therefore, along with, in spite of* are keys to the relationships between the ideas the author is presenting.

4. *Outlining* can come in handy when you're reviewing for a test. Group ideas so that their relationships are clear. This means making main categories under the general topic and organizing the specific facts under them.

5. *Notetaking* means organizing facts so they make sense to you. Make notes in your own words. Write down the important ideas, not just facts.

6. Here is one *notetaking technique*: Notebook paper divided into three vertical columns often works well. Use the large middle section for classroom notes, the left column for key ideas, and the far right column for textbook notes or a brief summary of the page you're studying.

7. *Remember assignments.* Keep a small assignment notebook. Assign a page for each day that work is due. Don't try to do a large assignment all at once. Break it into smaller tasks with one due each day, week, or month.

The Big Test and How to Take It!

If you can, think of the test as a learning experience and a chance to show how much you know about a subject.

1. Think positively.

2. Begin early. Study and review regularly.

3. Study by *self-testing*. Write down the questions you would ask if you were the teacher. Try to answer the questions after you close your book. Try different ways of answering, such as aloud, making a list, writing a paragraph, or outlining. Check yourself. This shortens study time and builds confidence.

4. Get plenty of sleep the night before. Eat breakfast.

Taking an Essay Test

1. Read the test all the way through before beginning.

2. Notice direction words such as *trace, list, compare,* and *discuss.* Be sure to do just what the directions tell you.

3. Choose one question with which to begin. It should be the one you find the easiest to answer. This will help you start remembering facts and give you confidence.

4. Remember that a well-written answer to an essay question begins with an introductory statement and ends with a concluding statement.

Building Good Study Habits (cont.)

5. Plan to have time to proofread your answers.

Taking a Short-Answer Test

1. Read each question carefully.

2. Move along at a steady pace.

3. Skip over any questions you're not sure of, and come back to them later. Mark them in some way so you won't forget.

4. Plan to have time to proofread your answers.

Developed by the Parent Center, Albuquerque, NM

Appendix C

- *Interest Survey — Parent Workshops*
- *Strengths and Needs Assessment*

Interest Survey — Parent Workshops

Please check a total of five (5) topics that would be of most interest to you.

General Topics for Parents of Students K-12

_____ 1. The Challenge of Being a Single Parent

_____ 2. Assertive Discipline — Creating a Positive Atmosphere at Home

_____ 3. Divorce and Separation — Effects on Families

_____ 4. Parent Roles in Sex Education

_____ 5. Stepfamilies — How to Live in One Successfully

_____ 6. Parent-Teacher Conferencing — Tips for Parents

_____ 7. Helping Children Build Good Study Habits

_____ 8. Getting the Help You Need When Your Child Has Problems in School

_____ 9. Self-Esteem — Helping Kids Feel Good About Themselves

_____ 10. Freedom and Control — Setting Limits for Children

Elementary Topics for Parents of Students K-5

_____ 1. Communicating with Children

_____ 2. Helping Your Child Develop Language

_____ 3. Spending Quality Time with Children

_____ 4. Home Activities for the Young Child

Secondary Topics for Parents of Mid and High School Students

_____ 1. Living With Your Adolescent

_____ 2. Drug and Alcohol Use and Abuse

_____ 3. Helping Your Child Plan His/Her Future

Special Topics for Parents of Special Education Students

_____ 1. Stresses of Parenting an Exceptional Child

_____ 2. Helping Siblings of the Handicapped

_____ 3. Sex Education for the Mentally Handicapped

_____ 4. Helping the Learning Disabled Child

_____ 5. The IEP Process — Legal Issues and Parent Role

_____ 6. Behavior Management Techniques for Difficult Children

_____ 7. Dealing With Professionals: Teachers, Therapists, Diagnosticians, Principals

_____ 8. Your Child Has Been Referred to Special Education — What does This Mean?

THANK YOU FOR YOUR TIME AND SUGGESTIONS!

Adapted from a survey used in the Albuquerque Public School System in 1984

Strengths and Needs Assessment
For Parents of Developmentally Disabled Citizens

NAME _____ ADDRESS _____

AGE _____ PROGRAM/TEACHER _____

To plan parent programs, we need to know what kinds of topics are of interest to you. Would you please take a few minutes to let us know how important you consider each of the following areas *and* how much you already know about that area. If you are a two-parent family, both parents are asked to fill out this form; just use two colors of ink. When you've completed this, please return it to _____

How much do you know about this?
1 = not much   5 = expert

Would you like to learn more about this?
1 = no   5 = definitely

1 2 3 4 5 (1)	How infants/young people grow and develop. . . what's normal?	1 2 3 4 5
1 2 3 4 5 (2)	Relationships between brothers, sisters, and other children.	1 2 3 4 5
1 2 3 4 5 (3)	How does language develop? Can I help?	1 2 3 4 5
1 2 3 4 5 (4)	Setting limits, discipline, and home responsibilities.	1 2 3 4 5
1 2 3 4 5 (5)	What can I do to help my child's motor development?	1 2 3 4 5
1 2 3 4 5 (6)	Can anything be done to make feedings and mealtimes easier?	1 2 3 4 5
1 2 3 4 5 (7)	Understanding "intelligence tests" and evaluation procedures.	1 2 3 4 5
1 2 3 4 5 (8)	What can I do at home to help my son/daughter?	1 2 3 4 5
1 2 3 4 5 (9)	What services are available in the community?	1 2 3 4 5
1 2 3 4 5 (10)	How can I work more effectively with the professionals who serve my son/daughter?	1 2 3 4 5
1 2 3 4 5 (11)	Parent-professional conferences — how can I get the most out of them?	1 2 3 4 5
1 2 3 4 5 (12)	Impact of a new child on the family.	1 2 3 4 5
1 2 3 4 5 (13)	Ways of explaining handicaps to children, relatives, and others.	1 2 3 4 5
1 2 3 4 5 (14)	Medical, dental, and nutritional needs of the disabled.	1 2 3 4 5

212

Strengths and Needs Assessment (cont.)

1 2 3 4 5	(15)	Funding and legislation for the handicapped.	1 2 3 4 5
1 2 3 4 5	(16)	Single-parent and step-parent issues.	1 2 3 4 5
1 2 3 4 5	(17)	Effective parenting and communication.	1 2 3 4 5
1 2 3 4 5	(18)	How children/adolescents change adult relationships.	1 2 3 4 5
1 2 3 4 5	(19)	Drugs and alcohol.	1 2 3 4 5
1 2 3 4 5	(20)	Human sexuality.	1 2 3 4 5
1 2 3 4 5	(21)	How to work more effectively with the school system.	1 2 3 4 5
1 2 3 4 5	(22)	Social relationships.	1 2 3 4 5
1 2 3 4 5	(23)	Hearing from other parents who have children with similar disabilities.	1 2 3 4 5
1 2 3 4 5	(24)	Understanding more about my child's disability.	1 2 3 4 5
1 2 3 4 5	(25)	If we have another baby, what are our chances of having another child child with a handicap?	1 2 3 4 5

I also know something about the following, and can help out by using these skills (e.g. music, carpentry, puppetry): _____

_____

_____

_____

Any other suggestions, ideas, or concerns: _____

_____

_____

_____

Thank you for taking the time to respond. Your suggestions will be used to plan future parent meetings.

Appendix D
Reinforcement Questionnaire

REINFORCEMENT QUESTIONNAIRE

Name: _____ Date _____

School: _____ Age: _____

Filled out by: _____

1. The things I like to do after school are _____
_____

2. If I had $10, I'd _____
_____

3. My favorite TV programs are _____
_____

4. My favorite game at school is _____
_____

5. My best friends are _____
_____

6. My favorite time of day is _____
because _____

7. My favorite toys are _____
_____

8. My favorite records or tapes are _____
_____

9. My favorite subject at school is _____
_____

10. I like to read books about _____
_____

11. The places I'd like to go in town are _____
_____

12. My favorite foods are _____
_____

13. My favorite inside activities are _____
_____

14. My favorite outside activities are _____
_____

15. My hobbies are _____
_____

16. My favorite animals are _____
_____

17. The three things I like to do most are

18. The three things I would like to have most are

19. The three things I like to do *least* are

Appendix E

- *Work Record Form,*
- *Point Record Sheet*

WORK RECORD

Week _____

Supervisor _____

	Monday	Tuesday	Wednesday	Thursday	Friday	Saturday	Sunday
1.							
2.							
3.							
4.							
5.							
6.							
7.							
TOTAL POINTS							

1.　　　　5.
2.　　　　6.
3.　　　　7.
4.　　　　8.

Total Possible _____

Total Earned _____

POINT RECORD

Date	Points Earned	Points Spent	Points on Hand	Points Spent for

Appendix F
National Service Organizations

NATIONAL SERVICE ORGANIZATIONS

ACCENT on Information, Inc.
P.O. Box 700
Bloomington, IL 61701

Alexander Graham Bell Association for the Deaf
3417 Volta Pl.
Washington, DC 20007

American Association on Mental Deficiency
5101 Wisconsin Ave. NW, Suite 405
Washington, DC 20016

American Cleft Palate Educational Foundation
Parent Liaison Committee
Louisiana State University Medical Center
Dept. of Audiology & Speech Pathology
3755 Blair
Shreveport, LA 20852

American Coalition of Citizens with Disabilities
1346 Connecticut Ave., NW
Washington, DC 20036

American Council of the Blind
1211 Connecticut Ave. NW, Suite 506
Washington, DC 20036

American Foundation for the Blind
15 W. 16th St.
New York, NY 10011

American Lung Association
1740 Broadway
New York, NY 10019

American Printing House for the Blind
1839 Frankfort Ave.
P.O. Box 6085
Louisville, KY 40206

American Speech-Language-Hearing Association
10801 Rockville Pike
Rockville, MD 20852

Association for Children and Adults
with Learning Disabilities
4156 Library Rd.
Pittsburgh, PA 15234

Association for the Education of the Visually Handicapped
206 N. Washington St.
Alexandria, VA 22314

Association for Retarded Citizens of the United States
2501 Ave. J
Arlington, TX 76011

The Association for the Severely Handicapped (TASH)
7010 Roosevelt Way NE
Seattle, WA 98115

Association of Learning Disabled Adults
P.O. Box 9722
Friendship Station
Washington, DC 20016

The Association on Handicapped
   Student Service Programs in Post-Secondary Education
Box 8256, University Station
Grand Forks, ND 58202

Boys Scouts of America, Scouting
   for the Handicapped Division
P.O. Box 61030
Dallas/Ft. Worth Airport, TX 75261

Cancer Information Clearinghouse
National Cancer Institute
Bethesda, MD 20205

Candlelighters Foundation
2025 Eye St. NW, Suite 1011
Washington, DC 20006

Coordinating Council for Handicapped Children
220 South St., Room 412
Chicago, IL 60604

Cornelia de Lange Syndrome Foundation
60 Dyer Ave.
Collinsville, CT 06022

Council for Exceptional Children
1920 Association Dr.
Reston, VA 22091

Developmental Disabilities Office
U.S. Department of Health and Human Services
200 Independence Ave. SW, Room 338E
Washington, DC 20201

Down Syndrome Congress
1640 W. Roosevelt Rd., Room 156E
Chicago, IL 60608

Epilepsy Foundation of America
4351 Garden City Dr., Suite 406
Landover, MD 20785

Federation of the Handicapped
211 W. 14th St.
New York, NY 10011

Friederich's Ataxia Group in America
P.O. Box 11116
Oakland, CA 94611-0116

Girl Scouts of the U.S.A.
Services for Girls with Special Needs
830 Third Ave.
New York, NY 10022

Goodwill Industries of America
9200 Wisconsin Ave.
Washington, DC 20014

Helen Keller National Center
for Deaf/Blind Youth and Adults
111 Middle Neck Rd.
Sands Point, NY 11050

International Association for Parents of the Deaf
814 Thayer Ave.
Silver Spring, MD 20910

March of Dimes Birth Defects Foundation
1275 Mamaroneck Ave.
White Plains, NY 10605

Mental Health Association
1800 N. Kent St.
Arlington, VA 22209

Muscular Dystrophy Association
810 Seventh Ave.
New York, NY 10019

National Alliance for the Mentally Ill
1234 Massachusetts Ave. NW
Washington, DC 20005

National Association for Visually Handicapped
3201 Balboa St.
San Francisco, CA 94121

National Association of the Deaf
814 Thayer Ave.
Silver Spring, MD 20910

National Association for the Deaf/Blind
2703 Forest Oak Circle
Norman, OK 73071

National Association of the Physically Handicapped
76 Elm St.
London, OH 43146

National Ataxia Foundation
6681 Country Club Dr.
Minneapolis, MN 55427

National Down Syndrome Society
146 E. 57th St.
New York, NY 10022

National Easter Seal Society
2023 W. Ogden Ave.
Chicago, IL 60612

National Hemophilia Foundation
25 W. 39th St.
New York, NY 10018

National Information Center on Deafness
Gallaudet College
Washington, DC 20002

National Information Center
  on Handicapped Children & Youth
1555 Wilson Blvd., Suite 508
Rosslyn, VA 22209

National Library Service for the
  Blind/Physically Handicapped
Library of Congress
1291 Taylor St. NW
Washington, DC 20542

National Multiple Sclerosis Society
205 E. 42nd St.
New York, NY 10017

National Neurofibromatosis Foundation
70 W. 40th St.
New York, NY 10018

National Rehabilitation Association
633 S. Washington St.
Alexandria, VA 22314

National Rehabilitation Information Center
4407 Eighth St. NW
Washington, DC 20017

National Society for Children and Adults with Autism
1234 Massachusetts Ave. NW, Suite 1017
Washington, DC 20005

National Spinal Cord Injury Association
369 Elliot St.
Newton Upper Falls, MA 02164

National Tay-Sachs and Allied Diseases Association
92 Washington Ave.
Cedarhurst, NY 11516

National Tuberous Sclerosis Association
P.O. Box 159
Laguna Beach, CA 92652

Orton Dyslexia Society
724 York Rd.
Baltimore, MD 21204

Osteogenesis Imperfecta Foundation
P.O. Box 428
Van Wert, OH 45891

Parents of Down Syndrome Children
11507 Yates St.
Silver Spring, MD 20922

People First National Inc.
P.O. Box 12642
Salem, OR 97309

Prader-Willi Syndrome Association
5515 Malibu Dr.
Edina, MN 55436

President's Committe on Employment of
the Handicapped
Washington, DC 20010

President's Committee on Mental Retardation
Washington, DC 20201

Recording for the Blind, Inc.
Anne T. McDonald Center
20 Roszel Rd.
Princeton, NJ 08544

Special Education Programs
400 Sixth St., Donohue Bldg.
Washington, DC 20016

Spina Bifida Association of America
343 S. Dearborn Dr., Suite 317
Chicago, IL 60604

Tourette Syndrome Association
41-02 Bell Blvd.
Bayside, NY 11361

United Cerebral Palsy Association
66 E. 34th St.
New York, NY 10016

Appendix G
Perception and Values Exercises

ACTIVITY 4 (p. 62)

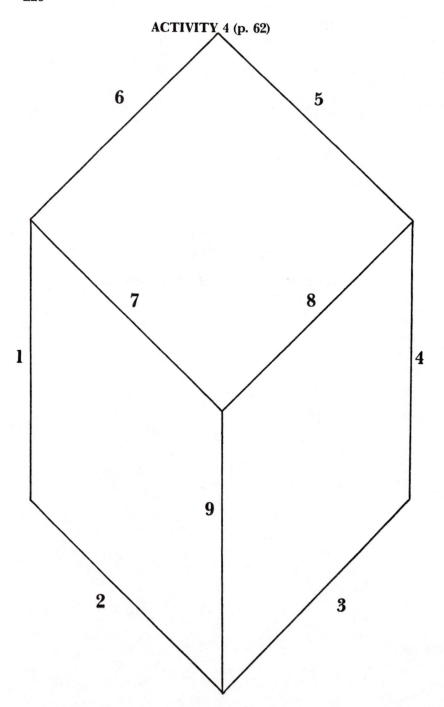

Activity 1:   Who Am I?

Dr. Manford Kuhn, sociology instructor at the University of Iowa, developed a free response instrument called "Who Am I?" One of the activities consisted of having the students take out a sheet of paper, head it "Who Am I?" and write down 20 statements about themselves. Dr. Kuhn felt that the items mentioned in answering that question could be considered as belonging to various personality types. At one time he was interested in the proportion of "consensual" statements to "subconsensual" statements. Consensual statements were those with clear boundaries that could be substantiated fairly easily by others, such as "I am a man"; subconsensual statements were much more subjective. While the analysis proposed by Kuhn may have value for the researcher, the activity itself can be meaningful to any individual.

Modified Procedure: Take out a sheet of paper, write down the date, and head it "Who Am I?" Now list as many things as you feel answer the question posed. For analysis purposes, you may want to reflect on the following questions:

1. Was this a difficult task to do?
2. Are you relatively satisfied with the things you listed?
3. Which items would you like to change? (You might want to place a checkmark by these.)
4. Would you like to add things to your list? (Jot these down.)
5. How many items relate to: Job? Family? Social life? Personal accomplishments?
6. From your list, can you tell anything about what you value?
7. If you were to give your list to a friend, would he/she recognize you and agree with your list?

Take your list and the analysis you made of it and put it away for a year. After a year has passed, do the activity again and compare the old list with the new one to see if you have changed. Reflect on why or why not.

Activity 2:   The Balance Scale

Justice is often depicted as a blindfolded woman holding an old-fashioned balance scale. In life, you probably like to do a number of things and do not like to do a number of things. Hopefully the scales of justice are tipped in favor of the "likes," but you may want to check this out.

Simon, Howe, and Kirschenbaum (1972) developed a strategy called "Twenty Things You Love to Do." The individual is asked to list things he/she loves to do and then code them as to when they were done last, whether they cost money, are done alone or with other persons, etc. The question that should be posed, of course, is: "Are you actually doing the things you really enjoy doing in your life?"

On the other hand, William James said, ". . . be systematically ascetic or heroic in little unnecessary points, do every day or two something for no other reason than you would rather not do it, so that when the hour of dire need draws nigh, it may find you not unnerved and untrained to stand the test" (1892, p. 149). You undoubtedly engage in a number of behaviors daily that you do not enjoy. You do them—but probably not for the heroic reasons James suggested.

Procedure: Draw a line down the middle of a sheet of paper, separating it into two parts. If you feel artistically inclined, you may want to draw a balance scale at the top, or you may want to cut out the zodiac sign for Libra and glue it at the top of the paper. On one side of the paper, write the heading "Things I like to do." On the other side, write "Things I don't like to do that I am currently doing." Now start listing activities in each of the columns.

When you have finished, consider the following questions:

1. Which column was the easiest to do?
2. Is your "like" column equal to or longer than your "don't like" column?
3. Are you doing or have you done recently those things you like to do?
4. Put a W for "work" beside items in each column that are associated with your job. Then look to see if your job has more things you like than you dislike.
5. Write a K beside items that involve some interaction with kids. Were there any? Should you be working with children?
6. How many of the "don't like" behaviors could you eliminate and still keep your job?
7. Put a P beside items that involve physical activity or are health-oriented. Are you keeping physically fit? Carkhuff and Berenson (1976, p. 22) indicated that the "helper must have a high level of physical energy if she or he is to discharge the demanding responsibilities of helping."
8. What "don't like" behaviors are you doing that are good for you (e.g., jogging or practicing a new skill that is difficult)?

You could do the balance scale activity from time to time to check for change or maintenance of behavior. In analyzing the lists, you may want to change some behavior. A program can be developed to deal specifically with certain items on the list. For instance, you may have listed playing tennis as a "like to do" activity, but realize that you have not played for months or years. Working out a schedule with a friend to play tennis regularly may help reestablish the behavior.

In some respects, having to program pleasurable activities seems a shame; yet, organization, planning, and structuring often allow more free time rather than less. Many writers set aside a fixed time to write, and musicians a time to practice. Some persons plan to ride horses, bicycles, or motorcycles every day. Others read for a while before they go to sleep. You should be able to learn new ways of behaving based on an analysis of your life style and the knowledge you have on how to organize and plan for behavioral change.

Activity 3: Are You a Teacher Who . . .

A number of years ago, Joel Goodman and Patty Bourexis devised an activity in which teachers were to check items that pertained to them in their interaction with children. This instrument could be used for self-analysis, or to check a persons's self-concept against another's perception of his/her behavior. Similar exercises are provided in *Discovering Your Teaching Self* by Curwin and Fuhrmann (1975).

Procedure: The accompanying chart is an adaptation of the instrument developed by Goodman and Bourexis. The format is the same, but the items have been changed to help you reflect more on your relationships with parents. In Column A place a checkmark beside the items that pertain to you. Then, if you want a check on how others see you, cover Column A or fold it under, give the chart to someone who knows you well (another teacher or supervisor), and have him/her mark in Column B. This is not as accurate as actually taking behavioral data on yourself, but if you can act on your values, others are usually aware of it. Column C can be used by a third person, or you can use it later to see if any changes have taken place.

You could employ a number of variations to the marking system suggested. For instance, you might use a U for "usually," S for "seldom," and N for "never" in marking Column A. The chart could be used by staff members in a school, responding individually. The aggregate results could be used for an inservice session on parent-teacher interactions. Teachers often like to discuss the relative merit of some of the items and reasons why they sometimes cannot do things they personally value. One teacher commented, "I really think it's important to visit in parents' homes, but we have a school board policy against it."

Are You a Teacher Who . . .

A B C

1. never admits to a parent that you're wrong?
2. has a sense of humor in a conference?
3. lets parents smoke in a conference?
4. offers coffee to parents during a conference?
5. doesn't have any favorites?
6. shows expression and emotions during a conference?
7. shows expression and emotions in parent groups?
8. starts conferences and parent meetings on time?
9. stops parent meetings at a scheduled time?
10. has contacts with parents?
11. has conferences in parents' homes?
12. compares students with their older siblings?
13. has trouble saying "I don't know" to parents?
14. talks less than 50% of each conference?
15. talks about your own problems and solutions in conferences?
16. sits behind a desk during conferences?
17. enjoys parent conferences?
18. has examples of children's work to show parents?
19. calls parents when things go well with their child?
20. sends notes home when children have behavioral problems?
21. uses grades to keep students in line?
22. has ever had a principal sit in on one of your conferences?
23. finds yourself criticizing more than praising your parents?
24. has ever had dinner at a student's home?
25. has ever had a parent over for dinner or a meeting at your home?
26. feels that parents have lost the respect of their children?
27. feels that parents have lost control of their children?
28. feels physically drained at the end of a series of conferences?
29. has parent group meetings?
30. has strong negative feelings about certain racial or sexual groups?
31. prefers to have conferences with fathers rather than mothers?
32. studies a child's folder and past achievements before a conference?
33. argues with parents?
34. feels intimidated by parents?
35. demonstrates to parents effective ways to work with their child?
36. likes to problem-solve with parents?
37. involves parents in planning for their child?
38. encourages parents to visit during class sessions?
39. uses parents as aides in the classroom?
40. does not want parents to teach their own children?
41. is honest with parents?
42. listens to parents?
43. dreads conference time?
44. invites parents to phone your home in the evening?
45. is positively reinforcing?
46. sends home daily or weekly report cards?
47. prepares handbooks or handouts for parents?
48. has a good attendance record at conferences and group meetings?
49. has students sit in on conferences with their parents?
50. talks about other teachers to parents?

Another said, "I don't think teachers should try to conduct parent group meetings with parents of children in their own classes. They can't open up because we hold their children's consequences."

You may want to ask yourself some of the following questions:

1. Am I really doing what I think I should be doing in my work with parents?
2. Does any research or objective data support or reflect the choices I have made?
3. Would the parents of the children I work with see me the same way I see myself?
4. Could I teach another teacher how to explore his/her attitudes and values in regard to working with parents?

Activities such as "Are You a Teacher Who ..." are easy to carry out and can be done independently. The list in the chart is not exhaustive. Other items can be added or substituted. You may want to develop your own list of behaviors that relate to consultant and teacher relationships. For many of the items, you could take behavioral data on yourself to test the validity of your response or to modify your behavior if change is desired.

You may want to share this activity with another teacher. If you are concerned with teaching, the chart itself should be a source of discussion. Feedback from a colleague about the usefulness of this technique should be valuable to you as a teacher.

Activity 4: There Ought to be a Law

You frequently hear someone say, "There ought to be a law against...." In a society that uses the law to guarantee rights rather than relying on dictatorial fiats, value systems are reflected in laws that are enacted. Citizens write and call their representatives and form lobby groups to promote values they feel strongly about and try to get them transformed into action. The rights of minority groups are ensured; the will of the people speaks. Currently, people are working to get thousands of laws enacted at national, state, and local levels.

Some laws reflect a moral philosophy that crosses national and cultural lines. The commandment "Thou shalt not kill," for instance, is fairly well respected in many nations, but it is seldom regarded as absolute. We in the United States consider killing permissible during times of war, in the line of duty, for self-protection, accidentally, and so on. Some say that education should be mandatory; others say it should be optional. Some believe books and movies should be censored or banned; others defend freedom of the press. Some are for capital punishment; others are against it. The disagreement in values continues with support from both sides.

Chances are that the laws you would like to see enacted reflect some of your strongest values. Suppose you could write at least four laws. What would they be?

Procedure: Take out a sheet of paper. Write, "Be It Hereby Resolved," and then write a law you would like to see enacted. It can be a new law or one that is already on the books. Try to write at least four laws, but feel free to give more. After you have completed the task, analyze your work by answering the following questions:

1. Would you allow any loopholes in your laws? For instance, if you wrote that "All children between the ages of 3 and 21 shall be provided a free public school education," does this mean that if a child tries to stab a teacher, he/she should still be provided an education? Does it mean that textbooks, annuals, caps and gowns, and the like should be provided?
2. Do your laws group themselves into certain areas of concern, such as health, education, or economics?
3. Do you think you could drum up much support for your laws from your friends? Do any groups already exist in agreement with your feelings?
4. Do you know of any laws that you think should be abolished?

This activity is a good one for creating group discussion. You will find yourself defending or decrying a position such as legalized gambling, decriminalization of marijuana, or compulsory education with little or no data. You will begin to ask yourself how the values you hold were formed.

Helping Others Assess Values

In addition to clarifying your own values, you should be prepared to help others with this process. The previous activities can be shared with co-workers, or they can be used in inservice sessions. Individuals, however, must not be put in the uncomfortable position of having to share before they are ready, or intimidated by a few people who are domineering.

A number of enjoyable activities that also illustrate that members of more or less homogeneous groups have different values are available.

Two of these activities, "Values Voting" and "Alligator River," are in Simon et al. (1972).

In "Values Voting" the leader reads a series of statements preceded by the words "How many of you." If the participants agree with the statement, they raise their hands; if they disagree, they put their arms by their sides; and if they have no opinion or do not want to commit themselves, they fold their arms across their chests. If the activity is carried out quickly, with a little humor, and without discussing any of the items, it can demonstrate the diversity of opinion in even a homogeneous group.

"Alligator River" is a story involving five characters, all of whom have some undesirable behaviors. The leader tells the story and then has the large group break into several small groups to arrive at a group consensus on how the characters should be ranked according to their desirability. After 10 minutes or so, the groups report back to the large group and discuss how the consensus was arrived at.

These exercises reveal that the teachers and parents with whom you work come to conferences and meetings with a wide range of values. You need to be aware of this phenomenon in order to work effectively. Individuals may become resistant if others ignore, refute, or put down their values.

The following activities are designed to be used by the significant others with whom you are working for the benefit of the child. Some of them can be used as individual exercises; others may be used to compare the values held between husband and wife or parent and teacher. In most cases they have been adapted from existing activities with some modification.

Activity 5:   Are You a Parent Who. . .

This activity utilizes the same format as Activity 3. The items, however, deal particularly with the parent-teacher relationship from the parent's point of view. A similar instrument could be developed pertaining more directly to the parent-child relationship and the values held regarding child rearing practices.

Procedure: The accompanying chart can be used in a variety of ways. One is to have the parent respond by putting checkmarks in Column A as he/she sees himself/herself. It could then be folded over for the teacher to respond in Column B. Another way would be for the wife to respond in Column A and the husband in Column B, and both to use Column C to check areas of agreement or disagreement. A third way would be to have the person record in Column A how he/she sees himself/herself, record in Column B how he/she wishes to be, and use Column C to record differences or things to be changed.

In addition to the analyses suggested above, parents may be asked to consider the following questions:

1. Why are the columns discrepant?
2. Are the discrepancies causing high degrees of friction?
3. Should specific behaviors be changed?
4. Do I know how to change the behaviors, or do I need additional help?
5. What have I learned about myself?

Many of the items can be used as discussion topics in group work with parents. Of particular interest are the discrepancies between husband and wife or between teacher and parent. Bringing these differences into the open may lead to new understandings and lay the groundwork for change.

Activity 6:   Whom Would You Tell?

This activity is similar to the Privacy Circle strategy discussed by Simon et al. (1972). It provides an opportunity for the parent to consider how open or closed he/she is in discussing handicapping conditions and other personal matters. No value is attached to openness or closedness, for as one mother said, "I might not mind talking about some of these things, but I must consider that my family has a right to privacy, too."

Benefits to exceptional children resulted from President Kennedy's speaking out about his sister who was mentally retarded, but this does not mean that all individuals should do the same thing. Each family must consider its individual needs and position in time. The exercise gives the respondent an opportunity to explore his/her own value system with respect to a limited number of family matters.

Procedure: This activity can be done individually or in a group. It can be analyzed by the individual through introspection, by the individual with a teacher or counselor, or used for group discussion. Give the checklist (page 236) to the respondent and ask him/her to place a checkmark in one of the columns for each of the 25 items. Explain that if "strangers" is checked, it means that the respondent would automatically tell all of the others. This should be mentioned, because sometimes you tell strangers things you would never tell your best friends.

Are You a Parent Who . . .

A B C

1. attends PTA meetings?
2. argues with teachers?
3. never admits to a teacher that you're wrong?
4. compares siblings with each other?
5. feels intimidated by school personnel?
6. admits to your child when you're wrong?
7. can listen to your child without interrupting?
8. dreads conference time?
9. calls the teacher when things are going well?
10. sends notes of appreciation to school personnel?
11. argues with your children?
12. displays your child's good work in prominent places?
13. feels in control with your child at home?
14. reinforces Board of Education members for appropriate action by letter or by phone?
15. has attended a workshop for parents?
16. volunteers as an aide in your child's class?
17. has invited your child's teacher to your home?
18. enjoys parent-teacher conferences?
19. criticizes the teacher or school to other parents?
20. feels school personnel have lost control of the children?
21. participates in educational planning at school for your child?
22. arrives at conferences on time?
23. tells teachers how to educate your child?
24. agrees with your mate on child rearing practices?
25. reinforces positively?
26. trusts teachers?
27. is fairly consistent in dealing with your child?
28. takes your child on field trips?
29. has trouble sleeping because of worry about your child?
30. feels physically drained after a weekend with your child?
31. says "wait until your father (or mother) comes home?"
32. feels that parents have lost the respect of their children?
33. has a sense of humor in respect to your child?
34. attends "special interest" parent meetings (ACLD, ARC, etc.)?
35. runs or helps run parent meetings?
36. tells children about your own problems when they try to tell you about theirs?
37. feels that school personnel are not entirely honest about children?
38. tells the principal when the teacher has done a good job?
39. calls the school if your child is going to be absent?
40. listens to the teacher during conferences?
41. attends outside activities for and with your child (e.g., scouts, athletics, music)?
42. enjoys playing games with your child?
43. has a picture of your child with you?
44. feels that few people other than you really understand your child?
45. asks the teacher what you can do to help your child at home?

236

Whom Would You Tell?

	Self	Intimates	Friends	Acquaintances	Strangers
1. Your child is a bed wetter?					
2. Your child lies?					
3. Your child is gifted?					
4. Your child has experimented with drugs?					
5. Your child has temper tantrums?					
6. Your child watches too much TV?					
7. Your child is mentally retarded?					
8. Your mate is under psychiatric care?					
9. Your child is brain damaged?					
10. Your mate is alcoholic?					
11. Your child has homosexual behaviors?					
12. Your unwed daughter is pregnant?					
13. You are having an extramarital affair?					
14. Your child was suspended from school?					
15. You slapped a child?					
16. Your salary?					
17. You have a blind child?					
18. Your exact weight?					
19. You smoke marijuana?					
20. You have a deaf child?					
21. Your method of birth control?					
22. Your child had run away?					
23. Your child is physically handicapped?					
24. You have a new car?					
25. Your child is learning disabled?					

This activity need not take long. After the task is completed, have the respondents consider the following questions:

1. Why do some handicapping conditions seem easier than others for me to talk about?
2. What is my "openness" score? By assigning a point value to each column (1 for "self," 2 for "intimates," etc.), the instrument can be scored. If a husband and wife engage in the exercise, they might want to compare their scores.
3. Have I learned anything new about myself as the result of this activity?

Using this instrument for research would be interesting. It has been suggested by some that fathers seem to be a bit more reserved than mothers in discussing various handicaps. The instrument has not been validated, but this area of values formation should be explored, particularly as work with parents becomes more common in special education.

Activity 7: Handicap Ranking Scale

Barsch (1969) developed a handicap ranking scale that he used with over 2,000 people including teachers, parents, and others who were involved with handicapped individuals. It was a list of handicapping conditions including polio and heart conditions, along with the more traditional categories. He asked the respondents to rank the conditions from most severe to least severe as to how the condition would affect the individual. Interestingly, parents did not tend to rank the handicap that their own children had as most severe, and teachers of the handicapped often did not rank the condition that they worked with as most severe. It was almost as if they were saying, "I know this condition, and it can't be as bad as _____." A blind student in graduate school marked blindness as 10 (least severe). When asked about it, she said, "I'm blind and I'm getting along fine. I'm just glad I don't have any of those other conditions." For purposes of this activity, the more traditional categories have been used.

Procedure: Hand the respondent(s) the handicap ranking scale, and have them rank the handicaps according to the instructions on it. Do not discuss the degree of handicap within the category; just ask them to respond from their own frame of reference.

After completing the task, discuss the following questions:

1. Was this a difficult task? Why?
2. What process did you go through to make your decisions?
3. Have you ever worked with anyone in the category you marked with a 1?
4. Do you think your ranking is fairly typical of how society at large would rank the categories?
5. Do you think society's ranking would have any effect on the funding of programs for the handicapped?

Data from a group of individuals can be aggregated for discussion purposes, or the individual can reflect on his/her own choices. This activity can be used with a PTA or any parent group, to explore attitudes.

Handicap Ranking Scale

_____ Elementary Age   Type of Handicap _____

_____ Secondary Age   Sex: M __ F __

Categories of handicapping conditions are listed below. Please rank these, from 1 to 7, according to *your own feelings*, on the basis of severity. Which handicap do you feel is the most severe problem a child could have? Which handicap do you feel is second most serious? Which do you feel is third most serious, and so forth. Consider only the individual and his/her problem in adjustment to school and life.

Handicap   **Rank**

1. Blindness   _____

2. Physical impairment   _____

3. Deafness   _____

4. Emotional disturbance   _____

5. Learning disability   _____

6. Mental retardation   _____

7. Speech/language impairment   _____

Activity 8:   Relating Domestic Values

In the late 1950s Farber, Jenne, and Toigo (1960) investigated the effect that a mentally retarded child had on the marital integration of husband and wife. One aspect considered in measuring marital integration was the ends the parents were striving for. This, the investigators felt, could be measured by looking at the consensus of husband and wife in their ranking of domestic values.

> Both husband and wife ranked a list of 10 domestic values in order of their perceived importance to family success. The list included (a) a place in the community, (b) healthy and happy children, (c) companionship, (d) personality development, (e) satisfaction in affection shown, (f) economic security, (g) emotional security, (h) moral and religious unity, (i) everyday interests, and (f) a home. (pp. 20-21)

As parents show an interest in exploring their own value system, a domestic values ranking activity might be explored.

Procedure: This activity can be carried out in a number of ways. One is to have the values listed on separate pieces of paper and have each partner put a number from 1 to 10 beside each of the values. When both are finished, you could take the lists of domestic values and on one sheet put the husband's ranking in one column and the wife's ranking in another. Then compare the differences.

Another way would be to have each of the values printed separately on a card. Have each partner rank the cards in order from most important to least important. When this is finished, take the original list and put each partner's rankings in separate columns for comparison. The card technique has the advantage of not implying an order at the beginning of the task. If you are so inclined, performing a correlation between the rankings is easy (Siegel, 1956). Then the parents could see the overall relationship between their rankings, as well as focusing on individual items that differ.

After the data have been compiled, the following questions should be discussed:

1. How did you feel about doing the activity?
2. Were you surprised at the results (i.e., the degree of agreement or disagreement)?
3. Have you discussed your differences or similarities on these values before?
4. What have you learned about yourself and your partner?
5. Are you satisfied with the results, or do you want to change? If you want to change, how might you go about it?

. The activity can be threatening, so you should be sensitive to the feelings of the individuals before, during, and after the activity. And you have to be ready to help the parents form a plan of action if they so desire. Agreements, one should remember, can be as important as differences. For some reason, many of us have become problem oriented rather than strength oriented. As parents, we respond to the lowest grade on the report card; as school psychologists, we respond to the valleys of the test profiles; and as teachers, we respond to bad behavior rather than appropriate classroom behavior. In working with significant adults, we must be constantly aware of the strengths that can help form the building blocks of a solid foundation for improved performance.

Activity 9:   Target Behaviors

The Q-sort was developed a number of years ago as a way of comparing a person's perception of his/her real self with his/her ideal self (Stephenson, 1953). It has since been used to compare perceptions of the significant others in a child's life (Kroth, 1973). The technique is simple, easy to explain, and quick to do.

Procedure: Use a form like the one on the accompanying page. List 25 target behaviors. The illustration form gives classroom behaviors, but any other behaviors at home or school could be listed.

Referring to the scale at the bottom of the form, Participant #1 should write in the value number associated with the behavior. For example, for Item No. 1, "Gets work done on time," Participant #1, the teacher, may feel that the child is "very much like me," and would then write the number 2 in the first box under "Real Sort."

After recording the value for each item on the "Real Sort," Participant #1 follows the same procedure for the "Ideal Sort," or how the participant would *like* the child to be — reflecting the value placed on each behavior. Then Participant #2 (say, the child) follows the same steps. (Two separate forms might be utilized, if the first participant's results might influence the other's. Then the numbers from one form could be transferred to the other form so they could be readily compared.)

Finally, the differences in perceptions and values are recorded by subtracting and recording these in the "Difference" column. The larger the number, the greater the difference. Items showing a great deal of discrepancy are targets for discussion or action.

These comparisons that can be made are innumerable: How the father sees the child versus how he would like to see the child; how the mother sees the child versus how the teacher sees the child; how the

Target Behaviors

Item No.	Behavior	Real Sort			Ideal Sort		
		Participant #1	Participant #2	Difference	Participant #1	Participant #2	Difference
1	Gets work done on time						
2	Pokes or hits classmates						
3	Out of seat without permission						
4	Scores high in spelling						
5	Plays with objects while working						
6	Scores high in reading						
7	Disturbs neighbors by making noises						
8	Is quiet during class time						
9	Tips chair often						
10	Follows directions						
11	Smiles frequently						
12	Often taps finger, foot, or pencil						
13	Pays attention to work						
14	Works slowly						
15	Throws objects in class						
16	Reads well orally						
17	Talks to classmates often						
18	Scores high in English						
19	Talks out without permission						
20	Rocks in chairs						
21	Scores high in math						
22	Asks teacher questions						
23	Uses free time to read or study						
24	Works until job is finished						
25	Walks around room during study time						

1 = most like me
2 = very much like me
3 = like me

4 = a little like me
5 = undecided
6 = a little unlike me

7 = unlike me
8 = very much unlike me
9 = most unlike me

father would like to see the child versus how the mother would like to see the child; and so on. The following questions may be asked upon completion of the activity:

1. Are we in overall agreement in how we perceive the child?
2. Are there similar goals (ideal sorts) for the child?
3. Where are the areas of greatest discrepancy?
4. Are the differences easily explained or are they going to be difficult to reconcile?
5. What have we learned about our perceptions by engaging in this activity?
6. Are there specific courses of action that should be taken?

As with the other activities that make comparisons between the values of participants, you should be ready to discuss similarities and differences. The participants may become defensive, which leads to difficulty in exploring and understanding each other's point of view. The teacher particularly should be wary of defensiveness as it relates to value sorting. If it happens, teaching becomes difficult because one tends to become authoritarian rather than understanding. For instance, a teacher may take the position that it is most important for the child to "smile frequently" and of little importance for the child to "score high in reading" at this stage of development, while the parent takes the opposite point of view. The teacher must take the lead in exploring and understanding these differences.

REFERENCES TO APPENDIX G

Barsch, R.H. (1969). *The parent of the handicapped child: A study of child-rearing practices.* Springfield, IL: Charles Thomas.

Carkhuff, R., & Berenson, B.G. (1976). *Teaching as treatment: An introduction to counseling and psychotherapy.* Amherst, MA: Human Resource Development Press.

Curwin, R.L., & Fuhrmann, B.S. (1975). *Discovering your teaching self: Humanistic approaches to effective teaching.* Englewood Cliffs, NJ: Prentice-Hall.

Farber, B., Jenne, W.C., & Toigo, R. (1960). Family crisis and the decision to institutionalize the retarded child. *CEC Research Monographs,* Series A (1).

James, W. (1982). *Psychology: A briefer course.* New York: Holt.

Kroth, R. (1973). The behavioral Q-sort as a diagnostic tool. *Academic Therapy, 8(3),* 317-330.

Siegel, S. (1956). *Nonparametric statistics for the behavioral sciences.* New York: McGraw-Hill.

Simon, S.D., Howe, L.W., & Kirschenbaum, H. (1972). *Values clarification: A handbook of practical strategies for teachers and students.* New York: Hart.

Stephenson, W. (1953). *The study of behavior: Q-technique and its methodology.* Chicago: University of Chicago Press.